# THE OFFICIAL
# MANCHESTER
# UNITED
## 1991 ANNUAL

# TOM TYRRELL

Macdonald
Queen Anne Press

A QUEEN ANNE PRESS BOOK

First published in Great Britain in 1990 by
Queen Anne Press, a division of
Macdonald & Co (Publishers) Ltd
Orbit House
1 New Fetter Lane
London EC4A 1AR

A Member of Maxwell Macmillan Pergamon Publishing Corporation

Design – Judith Clarke

British Library Cataloguing in Publication Data
The Official Manchester United annual.
  1991–
  1. England. Association football. Clubs: Manchester United Football Club. Serials
  796.3340942733

ISBN 0–356–19442–6

## PICTURE CREDITS

*Allsport:* 8, 13, 16, 24, 41B, 50–1, 69B, 74, 88, 92
*Associated Sports Photography:* 10–11, 58
*Bob Thomas Sports Photography:* 2–3, 12, 14–15T, 14–15B, 17B, 22T, 30, 39L, 39R, 47, 48, 67T, 68–9, 69T, 70, 72, 79, 83T, 89, 94–5
*Colorsport:* 18, 19T, 19B, 20–1, 27, 29T, 29B, 40, 45, 49, 52T, 53, 59, 62, 67B, 73, 75, 77, 83B
*Harry Goodwin:* 17T, 28, 32, 41T, 66, 76, 82
*Portsmouth Printing & Publishing Ltd:* 26, 31
*Press Association:* 80–1T, 80–1B
*Split Second:* 51B
*Sporting Pictures (UK) Ltd:* 25, 44, 52B
*Chris Tofalos:* 23

### Cover photographs

*Front:*   United skipper Bryan Robson (left)     *Colorsport*
            Match-winner Lee Martin hoists the FA Cup     *Bob Thomas Sports Photography*
*Back:*   Mark Robins is chaired off after scoring the winning goal in the FA Cup semi-final replay     *Colorsport*

Typeset by Acorn Bookwork Ltd, Salisbury
Printed and bound in Great Britain by Butler & Tanner Ltd, Frome and London

# CONTENTS

# *INTRODUCTION*

Here we go! The book every Manchester United supporter will cherish – your very own official Annual, packed with stories about your favourite club, and recalling that fabulous evening in May 1990 when the Reds lifted the FA Cup for the seventh time.

The book tells the story of the 1989–90 season with all its ups and downs, dramas and delights, and I'm sure you'll find it as enjoyable to read as preparing it for you was for me.

There can be no doubting that last season was interesting, to say the least. The Reds fought against relegation at one stage, and this after starting off their campaign as if they intended to win the title! There was drama behind the scenes, too, as the future of the club hung in the balance. There was big spending by the manager, and in the end those traumatic five days between the FA Cup final and its replay when Alex Ferguson made a decision which could so easily have cost him his job had it gone wrong.

It is at times like these that you realise what a difficult job it is to be in charge of a club as big as United, one which is constantly in the spotlight and whose fans demand the best, whatever the cost. Imagine what it must have been like for the United boss to tell Jim Leighton that he was not including him in the side to face Crystal Palace in that vital replay. Could you have done that? Could you have told someone you have known for years that you were leaving him out?

It was a trying time for Fergie, and he came through the test. He knew what he had to do, and he did it.

So United won the FA Cup, the seventh time they have done so, and Bryan Robson became, fittingly, the first captain to collect the trophy three times at Wembley. Now we have to look ahead, and the signs are there that Manchester United will rise once more.

By the time the next Manchester United Annual is on the bookshelves another season will have elapsed, and we will all have shared in its thrills and spills. Will it be the time for United at last to take that elusive League Championship? Will the young players who have begun to emerge finally claim permanent roles in the side? Will others arrive at Old Trafford to change the face of the side as the club strives for success?

Those questions will be answered in the course of time. Now, though, you can sit back and recall the moments that hit the headlines in 1989–90, remember the way that your favourites came through to finish with one of the game's top prizes, and perhaps dream of the day when someone somewhere will be reading about how you scored the winning goal in the Cup final . . . just like Lee Martin did when he read his favourite football book a decade ago.

**Tom Tyrrell**
*Manchester United Correspondent, Piccadilly Radio*

# TORMENT AND TEARS: WEMBLEY 1990

Alex Ferguson's first experience of an FA Cup final left him close to tears. His second left him holding the Cup after 24 hours of torment. 'That first ride up to the stadium in the team coach was incredible', said the United boss after the Reds had drawn 3–3 in a memorable game against Steve Coppell's Crystal Palace. 'I was choking back the tears when we turned into Wembley Way. The crowds were amazing, the whole place was a sea of United supporters, all of them urging us to do well. They wanted that Cup and they made their feelings known.'

*Players from both sides show their determination in the first episode of a dramatic final.*

'I don't want to upset the folks in Scotland, but I'm sure they'll understand when I say that leading out Manchester United for the 1990 FA Cup final was the greatest moment of my career. I have never felt anything like it, the noise, the emotion, the passion. I was almost crying when we drove up to the stadium and I filled up again as the crowd sang "Abide With Me" and the National Anthem. I don't think two sets of supporters have ever joined in like that.'

So began the first episode of a dramatic final, the outcome of which was not to be decided for another five days.

Wembley's first all-seater crowd for the best-known prize in the game witnessed a thriller in which two players from very different backgrounds took centre stage. Mark Hughes, the Welsh international who has played for three of the biggest clubs in Europe – Barcelona, Bayern Munich and United – and Ian Wright, who joined Crystal Palace from non-league football in his 20s, each scored twice as the game swayed one way then the other.

Palace led through Gary O'Reilly, who got his head to a free kick which appeared to hit Gary Pallister en route for goal, then Bryan Robson scored with a near-post header helped by a deflection from Palace full-back John Pemberton. Once level, United pressed forward and more chances came both before and after Mark Hughes scored his first goal of the Cup campaign, slamming in a low, right-footed shot in the 62nd minute.

Eight minutes later Steve Coppell sent Wright into the battle and the player who twice during the season had been out of action because of a fractured shin showed just why he is rated one of the top strikers in the country. His speed deceived United's defence and in the 73rd minute he rifled home a shot after cutting through the Reds' right flank.

Level again, the game went into extra time. Just before the end of the first 90 minutes Lee Martin had limped off with cramp, Clayton Blackmore taking

**Manchester United:** *Leighton, Ince, Martin, Bruce, Phelan, Pallister, Robson, Webb, McClair, Hughes, Wallace   Substitutes: Robins, Blackmore.*

**Crystal Palace:** *Martyn, Pemberton, Shaw, Gray, O'Reilly, Thorn, Barber, Thomas, Bright, Salako, Pardew   Substitutes: Wright, Madden.*

over. Then it looked as if disaster had hit the Reds. In the space of two minutes they were trailing 3–2 and had lost Gary Pallister. He went over on his ankle, hobbled off and was replaced by Mark Robins shortly after Wright had scored his second goal.

Palace were reaching closer for victory by the minute, United's defence was depleted and even semi-final hero Robins could do little to lift his colleagues: 'It was funny, though', Mark Two said later. 'When I came on I didn't think that we were going to lose, and after Sparky scored the equaliser I thought we had done enough to win it.'

Mark One scored his second with just eight minutes left, and it was sufficient to force a replay and a game which made headline news right from the kick-off.

Alex Ferguson decided to drop Jim Leighton and hand the goalkeeper's jersey to Les Sealey, the loan of whom from Luton Town was extended by two days after the final so that he would be eligible for the replay. There was also doubt about the injured Gary Pallister. Lee Martin, who had suffered cramp in both the semi-finals and during his first taste of a Wembley

match, was another problem for the United manager. Would Fergie gamble on Pallister's fitness, would Martin be too much of a risk?

Cramp had hit other players during the Saturday game, none more so than Paul Ince, who almost scored a dramatic winner during extra time yet suffered for his efforts. 'As I hit the shot I felt cramp coming on in my left leg. I fell over in pain and got cramp in my other leg. I didn't know which one to limp with!' said joker Ince, whose sense of fun fooled even the Duchess of Kent when the teams were presented to her after the drawn game.

'She held out her hand to shake mine, but I pretended that I didn't see her and was walking past leaving her holding out her arm. It's the sort of thing we do to our mates, and she took it as a joke when I stepped back and took her hand. The lads didn't see it, but my fiancée was watching and she did. She gave me some stick about it too, I can tell you!'

The day after the final United went empty-handed on a tour of Manchester aboard an open-topped bus, the homecoming having been arranged in advance.

*The replay. Bryan Robson heads under pressure from Palace's Alan Pardew.*

*Lee Martin beats Andy Gray on his way to the winning goal.*

Gary Pallister announced: 'I feel OK today, I think I'll be fine by Thursday'. In spite of his optimism, the 6 foot 4 inch defender needed a pain-killing jab before he took part in the replay.

On Thursday 17 May Wembley was packed once again as the United fans reacted to the stadium announcement that Jim Leighton was out of the side. Some looked shocked, others began to chant the name of Les Sealey. It was the only change to the team that started the game the previous Saturday. Both Martin and Pallister were able to play, and for one of them it was to be a night he would never forget.

Crystal Palace lost any friends they had made through their sporting approach in the original game as straight from the kick-off they stamped out their intent. They were going to kick United off the park! Players were booked as United were fouled on and off the ball and referee Alan Gunn had his hands full

keeping the game under control. Most of the aggression came from Steve Coppell's side.

The match was scrappy – there were stoppages every minute or so and at half-time the only scoring efforts had come from Neil Webb, who bent a shot into the side netting, and a Palace free kick, which Sealey did well to stop with his legs.

In the second half Palace's man-to-man marking began to go wrong and United broke away from the shackles. Neil Webb and Paul Ince showed their flair and holes began to appear in the Palace defence. Almost on the hour United flowed down the right wing, and Webb left defenders gasping as he stepped over scything challenges.

On the other side of the field Lee Martin was

**13**

sprinting forward, struggling to free himself from the attentions of close-marking opponents. Webb hit a right-footed cross. It was a precise, accurate pass. The ball floated over the heads of the Palace back four and into the path of Martin as he entered the penalty area. He met the ball, controlled it and hit a powerful right-footed shot which went between Martyn and his near post. It was a cruel, clinical kick, unstoppable by any goalkeeper. The ball hit the net to unleash an explosion of sound and Martin threw himself backwards to celebrate his goal and was buried under the bodies of his team-mates.

Lee Martin had found a permanent place in the history of Manchester United. He had scored the goal which won the FA Cup in a game he could so easily have missed!

The remaining minutes were dominated by United. Ince was the man of the match and Bryan Robson hit the crossbar with another scoring chance. As for goalkeeper Sealey, he did all that was asked of him and punched the sky with sheer delight as the final whistle went.

So the Cup was on its way back to Old Trafford to end a season of frustration and failure with triumph and tears.

United made their lap of honour as Palace players

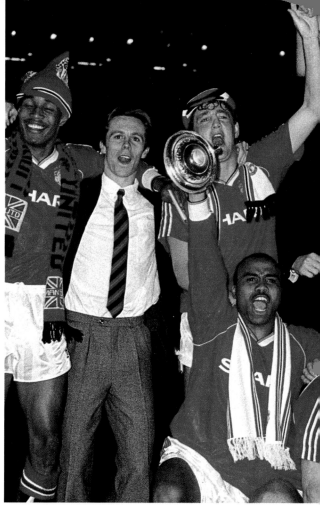

*We are the champions!*

left the field weeping openly. They had tried to bludgeon their way to glory and had paid the price. Few joined in their sorrow, but there was massive support for Steve Coppell as he walked away from the battleground.

As one, the United fans sang the chorus of the 1970s: 'Stevie, Stevie Coppell, Stevie Coppell on the wing', bringing tears to the eyes of the already distressed Palace manager.

And in the United dressing-room there were mixed emotions: tears of joy for those who had tasted success, and for Jim Leighton tears of a different kind.

*Fergie's gamble in fielding goalkeeper Les Sealey pays off – to the joy of both of them.*

# SECOND TIME LUCKY FOR LEE MARTIN

It was three days before the FA Cup final and the United players had gathered at a Cheshire Hotel to face the media for one last time before going off to their Wembley camp. For the experienced players it was nothing new. Bryan Robson and Neil Webb chatted confidently with the men from Fleet Street and the broadcasting companies, but for younger members of the squad like Lee Martin it was new ground.

'I've never even been to Wembley before', Lee said when asked for his experiences at the Empire Stadium. 'I've seen it on television, of course, but I have never been there and I just can't wait.' Little did he imagine what an important role he would play in the Cup final – let alone that he would get a second visit to the twin towers within the week!

*FA Cup glory for Lee Martin: only a week earlier he had yet to make his first visit to the twin towers.*

'What I'm looking forward to the most is just walking out on to the pitch down the players' tunnel. I've seen that so often on television and wondered what it must be like, now I have the chance to find out.'

The 22-year-old full-back is one of the quiet men of the squad who has forced his way into the side during the last two seasons. 'Really 1989–90 has been my first proper season with the first team. Before that I was in and out of the side, but this time I've played all the way through and it's terrific to end your first year at Wembley.'

A local lad, Lee lives in Glossop, a small town on the edge of the Pennines, close to Manchester although it is actually in Derbyshire. He has been connected with United for as long as he can remember:

'I came to Old Trafford as a schoolboy and began training with other players of my age when I was about 12. Then when I left school, the club took me on through the YTS scheme and eventually as an apprentice professional. I've actually been here for ten years – perhaps they'll give me a testimonial soon!'

He has no regrets about taking up his favourite sport: 'I always wanted to be a professional footballer and making it to the top with a club like United is something special. When I walked out at Wembley I knew that I was doing something every footballer in the country would like to do, and when I scored in the replay, that was incredible.'

'You always dream about scoring a winning goal in a Cup final, but that's all it is, a dream. When it happens in real life you find it unbelievable. I know I did it, but it took a long time to sink in. Even in the days after the game when everybody wanted to take my photograph and talk to me about the goal it didn't seem real. To have scored the goal which won the FA

RIGHT: *Lee realises his dream. He has scored the FA Cup winner at Wembley!*

Cup for your club makes you feel very proud.'

And the goal itself? 'Well, it was all down to Neil Webb. He laid on the perfect pass. As soon as the ball left his foot I knew where it was going to land, and I felt that I was going to score. All I had to do was run into the box and hit it. He put the ball right on to my foot.'

So one modest young man will always remember the 59th minute of the 1990 FA Cup final . . . and that second visit to Wembley which came so quickly after his first.

# RED DEVILS' DIARY: August

## Enter Mr K.

United fans looked forward to the start of the 1989–90 season with a certain amount of optimism. During the summer break Alex Ferguson had spent £2 million on Neil Webb from Nottingham Forest and Michael Phelan, the Norwich City captain.

There was every reason to believe that the Reds could get back to the form they had shown in 1987–88 when they finished runners-up in the Championship race. The next campaign had been disappointing, but it was obvious that the club was going through a transition period; established stars had left, new players were arriving. Could the final season of the decade bring that much sought-after title?

Our diary follows United's progress through a time when the club's off-the-field activities made as many headlines as the team's roller-coaster performances. It was a season of drama – right from day one . . .

*Michael Knighton displays his ball-juggling skills to the crowd gathered for the match against Arsenal.*

### Friday 18 August

What a way to start! On the eve of the opening game the news broke that businessman Michael Knighton was about to buy the majority share-holding in the club. Chairman Martin Edwards called a press conference at Old Trafford and the media gathered to witness United history being made.

What lay ahead for the club? Would the new man make changes, and if so, what would he do? What did the future hold in store for manager Ferguson and his players? Knighton was introduced as a man who would invest cash in the club and eagerly outlined his intentions, which included developing the Stretford End to the tune of £10 million. His plans would turn Old Trafford into the best stadium in the country, and there was talk of his cash bringing the superstars from the continent to play in our game. Could this mean Maradona and Robson in the same side?

Knighton told the world he was on his own in the venture and stole the headlines the following day as the Red Army gave him a rapturous welcome. He ran on to the pitch, waving to the cheering masses, and performed a ball-juggling act in front of the 47,000 gathered for the game against Arsenal. And this from a man who 24 hours earlier had claimed to be modest!

But Michael Knighton won over the fans in minutes and his pre-match entertainment helped to provide a carnival atmosphere for the big kick-off. Overnight Old Trafford had been transformed by a man who was unknown in football circles until that moment.

The showbiz start rubbed off on the players, who slammed champions Arsenal 4–1. New boy Neil

'Clearly this is a very big day in my life, but what I would like to say, and this is very important, is that Martin Edwards and myself have not just met, and it didn't just happen last night. We have reached a synergy together over the last six weeks, we've grown together as friends.

'I look forward to working with Alex Ferguson, he's got my 150 per cent support at the moment.

'I'm very anxious to make public from the outset that we intend completing this marvellous stadium we have at Old Trafford and making it literally one of the finest in the world – perhaps even the Mecca. Who knows? We've certainly got the legend to go with that.

'We will start immediately at the end of this season with the development of the Stretford End and certainly funds are in place to do that.

'Soccer is about commercial activity and about money. We are obviously on a very sound financial base already, we just need to promote that still further.

'As far as the players are concerned they will find me very human, a very ordinary man who is simply sharing the same passion for this marvellous sport as they do.

'Manchester United is internationally renowned and I intend to make sure that this legend continues. Yes, we will compete with the finest in the world.'

### Michael Knighton

*18 August*

*Skipper Robson congratulates a jubilant Neil Webb after his brilliant debut goal.*

Webb had a great debut, scoring with a brilliant shot ten minutes from full-time, and the crowd were ecstatic after seeing both Mark Hughes and Brian McClair add their names to the scoresheet following a Steve Bruce goal in the second minute. Immediately the experts began to talk about the Championship. Would this be United's year at long last?

Before curtain-up Fergie had been heavily criticised for selling Norman Whiteside and Paul McGrath, and the snipers were waiting for the chance to use this

*Mark Hughes (left) and new boy Neil Webb go for the ball. Both scored in the 4–1 defeat of Arsenal.*

against the United boss. Whiteside was popular with the United supporters, having come through the ranks to make it to the top, and while McGrath had slipped out of favour for his much-publicised off-the-field activities which led to a drink-driving ban, there were those who still saw him as an outstanding player.

Alex Ferguson knew he would be unpopular when McGrath was transferred to Aston Villa, but was prepared to face the consequences. When Everton signed Whiteside there were those who saw it as a mistake. But the success of Neil Webb in that opening game was enough to silence some of the hatchet men, and when United drew their second fixture, at Crystal Palace, there was little adverse criticism. Then the wheels fell off!

> 'I have a passion for United and I'd love to see the club win the League again. It seems to be the dream of every United fan and every United player at the moment, and I've still got friends connected with the club who were there when I was a player, so I would like to see them do well.'
>
> ### Steve Coppell
> Manager of Crystal Palace, 22 August

## Saturday 26 August

Derby County versus United at the Baseball Ground. Michael Knighton was at it again a week after his heading display; this time he appeared in the visiting directors' box as the Red Army descended on Derby.

Twenty-four hours earlier a newspaper article had named two other businessmen as Knighton's partners, claiming that they were the real money behind the take-over. Was his credibility now in doubt? Knighton strongly denied the report but admitted that he had approached a friend, Robert Thornton, after he had agreed the deal with Martin Edwards. Thornton had been asked if he wanted to become involved in the take-over.

Thornton was one of the duo named in the revelation and the fact that Michael Knighton had claimed he was on his own in the deal and yet seemed to have a partner began to throw doubt on the matter. Knighton insisted that he was pressing ahead with the deal using his own financial powers, but the media began to ask if Michael Knighton was all that he claimed to be.

As far as the terrace fans were concerned he was – there was no doubting his popularity as he smiled, waved and chatted with supporters at Derby. He strolled around the perimeter track, a man and his new football club together once more.

United supporters packed one end of the stadium and so many turned up that the kick-off had to be put back. Hundreds were led into the fenced-off zone behind the goal, and when youngsters began to climb on to the steel railings to get a better view, guess who asked them to get down so that the game could start? That's right, good old Mr K. – businessman, showman, peacemaker. More handshaking, more waves, more autographs for his new fan club.

But Michael Knighton could do nothing about the performance of the players, and the first defeat of the season saw manager Ferguson reaching for the chequebook as his critics reached for their knives. United put on an indifferent show and Dean Saunders gave the kind of display for Derby that can steal headlines, even from Michael Knighton.

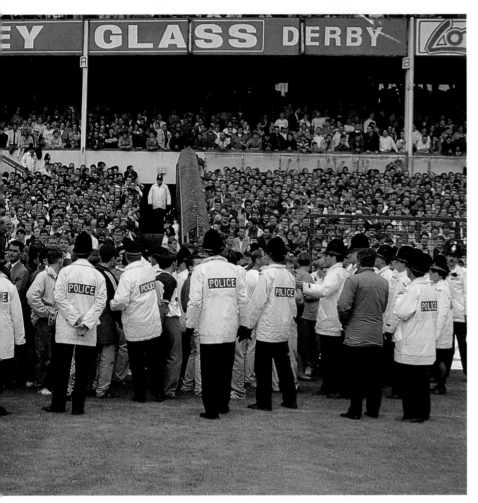

*So many United supporters turned up for the game against Derby that the kick-off was delayed.*

> 'What I said at the press conference last week is that I am the overwhelming beneficiary of my trust company, and I also said that when I have the time I will be inviting a few close friends to participate. That is precisely the case and I am frankly very irritated that some journalists don't quite understand the enormous power they carry to destroy a person's reputation with sensationalist headlines which are totally untrue. And I'm very, very annoyed with it.'
>
> ## Michael Knighton
>
> *26 August, after newspaper claims that he was not alone in the take-over bid and was being funded by business partners*

On the morning of the game there had been plenty written about United. They were linked with both Gary Pallister of Middlesbrough and West Ham's Paul Ince in what was set to be the biggest transfer coup in British football. The Ince deal was no secret – in fact, two months earlier the self-confessed United fanatic had been in hot water for having his photograph taken wearing a United shirt before anything had been agreed with his club. Ince had made it clear that his West Ham days were over and that he would only move if it were to Old Trafford.

## Monday 28 August

As the country enjoyed a sunny Bank Holiday United called another press conference, this time at the Ramada Renaissance Hotel in Manchester's city centre – plush surroundings for a transfer announcement, and perhaps fitting as United looked as though they were about to part with £4 million. Television cameras were set up and microphones positioned as the men and women of the media waited for the latest announcement. It had to be the double deal.

The cast entered: United officials, manager Fergu-

*Girlfriend Gillian congratulates £2.3 million signing Gary Pallister . . .*

son and Gary Pallister. The Middlesbrough player was introduced and shyly became the costliest signing in the domestic game. United had paid out £2.3 million for the 6-foot 4-inch defender.

But where was Paul Ince? The midfielder was nowhere to be seen, although his agent, Ambrose Mendy, was there as United revealed that the second deal had fallen through on medical grounds. Alex Ferguson had been ready to pay the Hammers £2 million, but now there was speculation about the future of the England Under-21 star.

Medical examinations had revealed a problem which, according to some sources, could have affected Ince's future. The next day, as Pallister met his new team-mates, Fergie claimed that the chance of the second deal being re-opened depended on the view of a Harley Street specialist. Agent Mendy hit out at United, saying that another medical examination had shown nothing untoward, and an on–off saga began as the Old Trafford medical advisers hinted at caution.

## Wednesday 30 August

United played bogey side Norwich City at Old Trafford and new boy Pallister gave away a late penalty to

*. . . but Paul Ince's celebrations were for another day – his deal fell through due to medical problems.*

| AUGUST RESULTS | |
|---|---|
| Manchester United 4 | Arsenal 1 |
| Bruce | Rocastle |
| Hughes | |
| Webb | |
| McClair | |
| Crystal Palace 1 | Manchester United 1 |
| Wright | Robson |
| Derby County 2 | Manchester United 0 |
| Goddard | |
| Saunders (pen) | |
| Manchester United 0 | Norwich City 2 |
| | Gordon |
| | Fleck |

### LEAGUE POSITION

| P | W | D | L | F | A | Pts | Pos |
|---|---|---|---|---|---|---|---|
| 4 | 1 | 1 | 2 | 5 | 6 | 4 | 15th |

Disappointment was in store for Gary Pallister in his debut against United's bogey side Norwich City.

hit the headlines again, but this time for the wrong reason. Worse than that, the Reds went down by 2–0, and also lost the services of skipper Bryan Robson.

He played only half of the game and it was obvious that he was feeling the effects of a heavy collision early in the match. More work loomed for the medical staff as the England captain was side-lined with badly-bruised ribs and out for a fortnight.

So after that wonder start United were left wondering what went wrong. Two successive defeats had given Fergie's critics the ammo they needed to get at him, and as the Knighton deal continued to hit the back and front pages the fans were bewildered.

United showed so much promise at the start of the

month, but now those who felt it might be the Reds' turn for the title were having second thoughts.

> 'I'm obviously disappointed with the result. As far as the penalty was concerned, I thought the ball was going out of play, and as I slid in on the wet surface Rosario went down and that was that, there was nothing I could do about it.'
>
> ### Gary Pallister
> *30 August, after his debut*

# *RED DEVILS' DIARY:* September

## *Webb's woe*

United had not made the best start to the new season, but things got even worse. Alex Ferguson discovered what it takes to be manager of the best supported club in the country – luck. His seemed to have run out as yet again a big-name signing was side-lined through injury. The Reds started the new month without Bryan Robson, who was still having treatment on that rib injury, and for Neil Webb, after just four games with his new club, disaster struck.

### *Wednesday 6 September*

After the Norwich game the First Division had a weekend off as England travelled to Gothenberg to play Sweden in a vital World Cup qualifier. As skipper Robson was injured, Neil Webb was the only player from Old Trafford in the squad.

He had a good game, but back home United supporters watching television were stunned to see him crash painfully to the ground while chasing a ball into the Swedes' penalty area. Webb was stretchered off, and back in the studio television expert Jimmy Hill predicted an Achilles' tendon rupture. He was spot on – for once! New boy Webb was to be out for months and there were even claims that he might not play again during the season.

Experts talk about the jinx on players signed from Nottingham Forest. Garry Birtles lost his scoring touch as did Peter Davenport, and back in the days of Frank O'Farrell Ian Storey-Moore played only 43 games before injury ended his career. No Webb, no Robbo and, with several of his young players injured, Alex Ferguson stepped up the interest in Paul Ince again. Would United gamble by buying a player who might be another injury risk?

Michael Knighton continued to make the headlines but it was a change of role for the man who had

*A major blow for United: Neil Webb is carried off injured during England's match in Sweden.*

planned to revolutionise United. Many newspapers predicted that he wouldn't come up with the cash to complete the deal. He stood firm, maintaining that all would become clear soon. The uncertainty started rumblings among the supporters but there was more than that to come to upset United followers.

### *Saturday 9 September*

As fate would have it, the first game of the new month was at Goodison Park, where United faced Everton and old boy Norman Whiteside for the first time since his controversial move. The same Norman Whiteside without doubt would have filled the midfield gaps had he still been at Old Trafford.

Everton looked set to run up a big score as first Newell scored, from a Whiteside flick-on, and then Nevin and Sharp rubbed in the salt early in the second half. United trailed 3–0 and the bubble seemed to have burst. Then came a spirited fight-back led by young substitute Russell Beardsmore. Brian McClair pulled one back and nine minutes later Beardsmore got a second, but Everton hung on to win 3–2.

Another defeat and, to make matters worse, Whiteside had had a great game. It was just what the headhunters wanted and more than many supporters could take. Whiteside refused to comment when asked about playing against his old club. Silence can say many things.

Played four, won one, drawn one, lost two – not the best way to go for the Championship!

The Knighton saga continued to unfold as the rumours prompted what seemed to be a campaign against him by some newspapers.

## Wednesday 13 September

Fergie stole the spotlight away from talk of the takeover as Paul Ince was finally signed in a deal dependent on his fitness. United had originally agreed to buy him for £2 million but, because of the doubt thrown up by medical reports, West Ham boss Lou Macari was willing to accept £850,000 and further payments geared to Ince's appearances. It was reported that every time Ince plays West Ham get a cheque for £5,000!

## Thursday 14 September

The spending didn't stop there. No sooner was the ink dry on Ince's contract than out came the chequebook again and another £1.2 million was on its way to Southampton's bank account as Danny Wallace joined the Reds. He was signed too late to play in the next game, but suddenly it was back to winning as Millwall came to Old Trafford as joint leaders of Division 1.

## Saturday 16 September

A date to remember. Seven days later came another, but for very different reasons. Ince had an impressive debut although he played for only 58 minutes. By the time he left the field United were leading 3–0 and still the scoring hadn't stopped.

Mark Hughes got two more to complete a hat-trick for the first time since his return from Barcelona, which was just what the fans wanted. The other goals came from 'Captain Fantastic', back from the rib injury, and young Lee Sharpe, who netted his first ever. 5–1 – remember that score. It was Fergie's biggest League win as United boss and gave him something to celebrate.

*Hot on the heels of Paul Ince, another new boy arrives: Danny Wallace greets supporters after signing for the Reds.*

## Wednesday 20 September

A month into the season Michael Knighton announced that it was all systems go. He now had the cash even though his original backers had pulled out and caused such a stir. The deal was to be unconditional, which meant that neither Edwards nor Knighton could back down without the consent of the other. A bit too complicated for the average fan – all he wanted was success on the field.

> 'I've got very mixed feelings about the takeover deal becoming unconditional. In one sense it's very sad, because I've been in the chair for nearly ten years and it's a big wrench to give that up. On the other hand, the reasons that I did the deal in the first place still stand. Michael Knighton is still prepared to put money up, or to back the development of the Stretford End to the tune of £10 million. He's already made that commitment and that was something which was a long way down the road had I remained in the chair.
> 'At the end of the day had the club remained in my hands it would not have worried me unduly.'
>
> ### Martin Edwards
> 20 September

*Paul Ince, who added his name to the score-sheet, battles away against Portsmouth.*

He got it – or seemed to. The Knighton announcement came on a day when United were in Portsmouth, and the man who hoped to be chairman flew south to watch the Littlewoods Cup tie.

Ince was joined by new boy Wallace in the line-up and they both put their names on the scoresheet as United played impressively, sweeping into a 3–0 lead by half-time. But the gloom descended again: Bryan Robson limped off, Pompey fought back and in the end United were lucky to take a 3–2 lead into the second leg.

Robbo's injury was diagnosed as a hair-line fracture of the shin, which takes several weeks to mend. So there would be no Robbo for the Manchester derby at Maine Road. Also injured was Steve Bruce, who had thus ended a remarkable run of four years of senior football without missing a match through injury.

After their stuttering start United were in mid-table and the win over Millwall plus the victory at Portsmouth made them favourites against City, who were struggling at the foot of Division 1.

## Saturday 23 September

What an upset! City ran riot and recorded their biggest ever win over United at Maine Road – 5–1. The Blues led 3–0 at half-time before Mark Hughes gave United

> 'Perhaps City wanted the win more than we did and we're disappointed that we didn't perform for our supporters. There's nothing I can say to comfort them, they will have their own opinions about today's game and I'm sure they'll be as upset as the players. They came and did their best to get the team going and we didn't respond. It wasn't the greatest baptism as captain of Manchester United.'
>
> ## Michael Phelan
>
> *23 September, after standing in as skipper for the derby game at Maine Road*

> '*I don't think that the speculation about my future is personal, I think it's just because I'm manager of Manchester United, and people in this job have always been the whipping boys for the press. Really there is nothing that you can do about it and I've just got to get on with the job and have a smile on my face about it all.*
> '*I know that I'm doing my job properly and I'm doing it honestly, and there's no manager in this county who could do the job better than me. I know that, and people within this club know that, and that's probably why our directors have given me a new three-year contract – they recognise what's been achieved. This is not a blow-your-own trumpet situation, I think the facts are the facts.*
> '*It's a hard job and I'm doing it to the best of my ability.*'
>
> *Alex Ferguson*
> 29 September

saved United from another defeat hot on the heels of the derby humiliation. But television dictating the fixtures? Was this a sign of things to come?

*Fergie's job was not made any easier in September by critical reports in the press.*

fans some hope by scoring his fifth of the season with a spectacular overhead kick. It was the goal of the game, but that was no real consolation. Danny Wallace fired in a shot, and City cleared downfield to score their fourth. The rout was completed with a fifth – and there were still 29 minutes left.

Manchester was no place to be for those preferring red to sky blue, and the City fans were given a very different reason for remembering derby day 1989 than were their Old Trafford counterparts.

This latest defeat was all the hatchet men needed. Speculation mounted about the future of Alex Ferguson as back page headlines screamed for his head. Howard Kendall, one-time manager of Everton, and then with Atletico Bilbao, was linked to the job – it was rumoured that he was not enjoying life in Spain. But Fergie stood firm and told the world that he was the best man for the job. He was confident that United would pull out of the doldrums and that, given time, his big spending would pay dividends. Time will tell if he was right.

## Saturday 30 September

Another blank weekend – United's game at Anfield was called off, not because of the weather, but because television chiefs decided that it would make a screen spectacular just before Christmas. The new date for the fixture – Friday 22 December – perhaps

### SEPTEMBER RESULTS

| Everton 3 | Manchester United 2 |
|---|---|
| Newell | McClair |
| Nevin | Beardsmore |
| Sharp | |

| Manchester United 5 | Millwall 1 |
|---|---|
| Hughes (3) | Sherringham |
| Robson | |
| Sharpe | |

| Manchester City 5 | Manchester United 1 |
|---|---|
| Oldfield (2) | Hughes |
| Morley | |
| Bishop | |
| Hinchcliffe | |

### LITTLEWOODS CUP: Second Round 1st leg

| Portsmouth 2 | Manchester United 3 |
|---|---|
| Black | Ince (2) |
| Kuhl | Wallace |

### LEAGUE POSITION

| P | W | D | L | F | A | Pts | Pos |
|---|---|---|---|---|---|---|---|
| 7 | 2 | 1 | 4 | 13 | 14 | 7 | 14th |

# PAUL'S AIM: 'I'D LIKE TO BE CAPTAIN'

Paul Ince could never be described as a man without ambition. He set out his stall early in the summer of 1989, when managerial turmoil at West Ham saw the departure of John Lyall. Paul declared that he wanted to play for his favourites, Manchester United . . . and when he eventually signed for them he said that one day he hoped to be skipper! If his determination to join United is anything to go by there is every reason to believe that the midfield star will achieve his goal.

Paul signed for United on 13 September 1989 but had no qualms about the date: 'It's a lucky day for me. I've finally got here and I can't wait to pull on a United shirt and get out in front of those supporters. This is the biggest and best club in the country, and to be part of it is a tremendous feeling'.

Paul's transfer from the East London club was beset by problems, and at one stage it looked as if his hopes of playing for the club he had supported as a small boy were going to be shattered. 'When I was nine I was Manchester United daft', says Paul, who was born in Ilford and until his move north had spent his life in the London area. 'That wasn't unusual because at that time there were a lot of exciting things going on at Old Trafford. It was in the days of Tommy Docherty, when there were players like Steve Coppell, Gordon Hill, Stuart Pearson and Sammy McIlroy in the side.

'Kids like to support a winning team, and after United beat Liverpool in the 1977 FA Cup final they were the club for me. I had pictures of the team on the bedroom wall, I had a United strip and if you asked me who I wanted to play for the answer would always be "Man U". But as I got a bit older and more into football and the chance of playing for West Ham came along. I'm afraid all my United stuff went out of the window!'

Understandably, Paul became a West Ham fan, and when he made it into the first team it was an ambition achieved. 'To play for the team you have watched as a teenager is a big thrill. Any player will tell you that as a kid he wanted to play for a certain team,

and to actually do that is something special.'

However, it all started to go wrong for Paul when the long-serving John Lyall was sacked by the Hammers. Like many of the players, he had only worked under one man and the changes at Upton Park, coupled with the news that Manchester United were interested in him, made Paul determined to get away. 'Footballer's lives are short, and you have to take any opportunity which comes along. Some of the West Ham fans turned against me, especially after there were problems with the deal, but there were those who were more understanding.'

Paul was due to sign for the Reds on 28 August in a record-breaking £4.5 million double package. He and Gary Pallister were set to join United at a signing ceremony staged in a city centre hotel. Television cameras were set up, microphones were in place and the media were gathered to witness the joint signing . . . Gary was there but Paul was missing.

He was stunned to be told that there were medical problems, and that United were having second thoughts about the deal. 'It was the worst moment of my life. I hadn't played for a few weeks because of the problems at West Ham, and I had a slight injury, but I felt fine. I didn't think that there was anything seriously

*A dream realised: Paul wears the United shirt at long last.*

*The determined Paul Ince puts Sheffield United through their paces.*

wrong with me, yet the medical experts were telling United to have a closer look. I began to wonder what their examination had revealed', he says.

Other opinions were called for and it looked as if the ambitions of Paul Ince would be rudely curtailed. In between the sacking of John Lyall and the United approach Paul had upset West Ham fans by having his photograph taken for a newspaper wearing a Manchester United shirt. He had declared that he would never play for the Hammers again – now it seemed that he would have to go back to Upton Park and eat humble pie.

For the next 16 days the transfer was off and then on again. The tabloids had a field day. Conflicting stories abounded: there was nothing wrong with Ince; United were trying to bluff West Ham into dropping the agreed price; the Reds would be foolish to try to pursue the deal. Then came the breakthrough, and Paul moved to Manchester.

The clubs agreed to a staggered payment deal, United paying West Ham as Paul proved his fitness. Paul Ince signed for United and had one of the strangest ever introductions. Normally, when a new player is recruited, the club holds a press conference followed by the traditional pictures on the Old Trafford pitch of the player holding aloft a United scarf. For Paul Ince there was little razzmatazz.

Those lucky enough to discover that the deal had gone through interviewed him in the club car park, where a handful of surprised supporters on a ground tour witnessed the proceedings! But what mattered was that he was finally a United player. 'I'm glad that it's all over. These last few days have been terrible for me, wondering whether or not I'd be coming here.

'Now all I want to do is settle down in this area. I hope to get married next year, and finding the right place to live is very important. I want to establish myself in the team, and I can't wait to get playing again. Obviously all the publicity surrounding the transfer has been a bit worrying, but that's all over now. I had some great days at West Ham, and some of the supporters there have wished me luck. They would have done the same thing if they had been given the opportunity. As for the others . . . well they can get lost!'

One ambition achieved, then, but what about the next? 'Well, I'd like to win something with United, I'd like to get myself into the full England side, and perhaps one day I'd like to be captain of United. There can be no better feeling than leading them out.'

*And win something he did. Just watch Paul Ince as he goes for ambitions three and four!*

# RED DEVILS' DIARY: October

## A miracle for Robbo

Everything in the garden was far from lovely as United entered the third month of the new season. They were in 14th place, sixth from the bottom, and home performances had left a lot to be desired. But for those with hope there still seemed to be a chance of revival. The gap between the top and bottom of the table was represented by only a handful of points, three wins in a row could move virtually any side to the top . . . could that be United?

Fingers were being pointed at Fergie for his big spending, and because his new squad seemed unable to find consistency, but the Reds' boss was unmoved. He knew it was going to be tough and he was ready for it.

According to many supporters the Knighton affair had had its effect on the players, but Alex Ferguson and his squad denied this. However, as the new month began, there was good and bad news for the club. The bad: Edwards versus Knighton in the High Court; the good: Bryan Robson was back.

*One piece of good news amid October's traumas was skipper Robson's amazing recovery.*

### Monday 2 October

Fergie stunned everyone by declaring that Robbo would play against Portsmouth in the forthcoming Cup tie. The England skipper had been side-lined since the first leg of the Littlewoods Cup clash with an injury diagnosed as a hair-line fracture of his shin. An X-ray revealed the damage, and time was felt to be the only healer.

But two weeks after limping out of the game at Fratton Park Robbo reported back for full training. Apparently he had been to see a woman who cures ailments and injuries through the 'laying on of hands' and she mended his leg! A miracle cure? It certainly looked that way.

### Tuesday 3 October

United scraped through against a lively Portsmouth side in a 0–0 second leg watched by a far from satisfied crowd. The fans aired their grievances as they walked out of Old Trafford, many season ticket-holders accusing chairman Edwards of upsetting things because of his decision to sell out.

United had plenty of chances but could not beat Alan Knight in the Pompey goal, and there were one or two narrow escapes at the other end before the final whistle saw United through to the next round.

It was smiles all round 24 hours later when the draw for the third round was made on television. United

*Mark Hughes is on the attack, but United could only manage a 0–0 draw at Portsmouth as controversy raged off the field.*

were to be at home to Tottenham Hotspur – the plum of the competition. Surely this would be the game to lift the depression? United would have home advantage, but it remained to be seen.

## Wednesday 4 October

The Knighton saga continued – journalists were camped out at Old Trafford today and for the next three days as events took another dramatic turn. There were stories that Knighton was trying to 'hawk' the club, offering it for sale to the highest bidder.

United's directors were far from happy, and let their feelings be known when they turned up for daily meetings at the ground. Then the saga became a legal battle as Edwards took Knighton to court.

> 'All the directors of the club are true United supporters. They've all got Red blood and they are all totally humiliated and embarrassed by the current position. There have obviously been legal constraints upon us because of the contract between Martin Edwards and Mr Knighton, and we haven't been in any position to do anything up to now, but at the moment we are examining all the possibilities and we hope we'll be able to make an announcement later.'
>
> **Michael Edelson**
> vice-chairman, 5 October

## Thursday 5 October

Edwards served an injunction on Knighton to prevent him from leaking confidential information on the club's financial position and the take-over details.

It was way over the head of the average fan, who simply wanted to see his side winning games, but as the saga continued the back and front pages were full of differing versions of the story. Some claimed that Mr K. had made United the laughing stock of football.

## Friday 6 October

Newspaper magnate Eddie Shah created a sensation by revealing in an interview with the Annual's editor, Tom Tyrrell, broadcast on Manchester's Piccadilly Radio, that Knighton's representatives had offered him a stake in the club at a profit. He claimed that it became clear to him during discussions that the man who told everyone he was entering football because of his love of the game was only in it for the money.

Knighton was ready to buy the Edwards share-holding but was willing to sell it for personal gain!

Shah said that Knighton's representative had shown him papers of a confidential nature that he felt he should not have seen. He had held on to them after explaining that he wanted his advisers to have a closer look, but instead returned them to Martin Edwards. The plot thickens!

*October saw more troubled times for chairman Edwards.*

## Tuesday 10 October

As United's directors continued their daily meetings and the media became as bored with the saga as the supporters, talks suddenly switched to a city centre hotel, where in the early hours of the morning Martin Edwards and Michael Knighton came to another agreement.

It all took place at a time when, according to take-over rules, every United share-holder should have been about to be mailed an offer for his or her stake in the club. If Martin Edwards was getting £20 a share, then Joe Bloggs had to get the same offer whether it was one share or a thousand.

The mail-out had to be made by midnight tonight . . .

## Wednesday 11 October

No mail-out, no offer to every share-holder, but it looked as though it could finally end today.

The late night talks went on too long for the newspapers to carry the outcome, but it seemed as if matters would come to a head when a press conference was called at Old Trafford. The press gathered for a late morning announcement, but it didn't start on time.

There was a shuffling of feet as first coffee then sandwiches were served, then more coffee, and more sandwiches. Journalists looked anxiously at their watches as deadlines approached and departed. Still nothing. Then, late in the afternoon, Messrs Edwards and Knighton entered, apologising for the delay which had been caused by lengthy legal talks.

After days of speculation the take-over took a sensational twist. The contract under which Edwards was to sell his 50.06 per cent holding to Knighton's company, M.K. Trafford Holdings Ltd, had been cancelled by mutual consent. Knighton had pulled out of the deal but he became a director of the club.

Knighton bravely faced questions and ran the gauntlet well. He made it clear that he had the cash to complete the deal but felt that it would not have been in the best interests of the club to carry it through. Was it over at last?

As the club rocked in the eyes of many, attention switched to England's World Cup qualifier against Poland, and Captain Robson led his side through to the finals in Italy.

## Saturday 14 October

Terrace talk was still about the Knighton affair and it was obvious that Mr K. was no longer as popular with the fans as he had been at the start of it all. Then somebody remembered football. Football. . . .!

The fixture list had thrown up a beauty. United versus Sheffield Wednesday, struggling at the very bottom of the First Division, and managed by none other than Ron Atkinson, the man Alex Ferguson replaced in November 1986. It was his first visit to his old club as a rival manager.

Big Ron's side forced a 0–0 draw and that brought more frustration for the Old Trafford faithful, whose patience is running short. The 'boo-boys' were warming up and Knighton got his share of the criticism, although a two-hour appearance on a radio 'phone-in before the game had eased things a little as he talked his way through his side of the story.

A week later it was very different.

> 'Obviously the players have been concerned about what has been happening during the take-over situation because it does affect us as players at the club, but we try not to let it affect us on the pitch. The lads talk about it and we read different stories in the newspapers, and that's all we know about it. You can do without all the adverse publicity but when people say to me that Manchester United has been dragged down into the gutter I don't agree. I think things have gone on too long and people have made a lot of it because it is United, but we never felt laughing stocks. It got a bit messy and maybe it should have been resolved a lot quicker than it was, but it's not for me to say.'
>
> **Bryan Robson**
> *14 October*

## Saturday 21 October

A glorious show at Coventry saw the first away League win of the season and the new players really did strike a blend. A Steve Bruce pipe-opener was followed by two from Mark Hughes and a first ever goal by Michael Phelan, who was celebrating his call-up to the England squad. United won 4–1, the perfect springboard for the Littlewoods Cup. The players ran across to the Red side of Highfield Road to applaud the fans at the end.

But the roller-coaster ride continued: four days after Fergie's biggest away win since his move south of the border came his biggest home defeat.

## Wednesday 25 October

A big crowd packed Old Trafford for the third-round tie with United's home advantage providing plenty of optimism in the night air. Spurs were without Paul Gascoigne and were struck a further blow in the 13th minute when Terry Fenwick was carried off with a broken leg after a tackle on Mark Hughes.

It became the turning point of the game as Spurs changed their tactics. Defender Fenwick was replaced by Paul Moran and a reshuffled Tottenham went all out for goals. First Lineker then, just after half-time, Samways and finally Nayim made it a gloomy night for United, who came close but not close enough.

Beaten 3–0 and with their League form looking bleak it seemed as though this might not be a season of success after all.

Now that the Knighton affair had been swept out of the back pages there came another sensational head-line. Bryan Robson was wanted by Marseilles, who were willing to pay United £4 million for their star. Fergie said he was not for sale at any price, even though such a move would have made Bryan financially secure for the rest of his life.

The story left some pundits claiming that £4 million in the bank might have been a sound investment, and others that Robbo has eyes on the manager's job should it become available.

## Saturday 28 October

After the gloom of midweek the month ended on a high note as third-placed Southampton arrived at Old Trafford ready to take on all comers.

Danny Wallace missed the chance of playing against his old pals because of a hamstring strain, but the United fans got the chance to see one of his

brothers in action. Rodney Wallace played his part in the nip-and-tuck game, while the third Wallace – Ray – sat on the Southampton bench.

Brian McClair began the scoring in the 16th minute only for Saints to level 60 seconds later. Was it to be another of those afternoons? No, United battled all the way and McClair got another in the 61st minute to take the points.

United moved to 11th in the table but only six points from top spot. Could this be the revival the fans had been waiting for?

The players looked as though they were beginning to knit together and with only ten League games completed there remained enough of the season for that challenge. Perhaps those dreams of the title could still come true.

---

## OCTOBER RESULTS

| | |
|---|---|
| Manchester United  0 | Sheffield Wednesday  0 |

| | |
|---|---|
| Coventry City  1 | Manchester United  4 |
| Drinkell | Bruce |
| | Hughes (2) |
| | Phelan |

| | |
|---|---|
| Manchester United  2 | Southampton  1 |
| McClair (2) | Le Tissier |

### LITTLEWOODS CUP:  Second Round  2nd leg

| | |
|---|---|
| Manchester United  0 | Portsmouth  0 |

### Third Round

| | |
|---|---|
| Manchester United  0 | Tottenham  3 |
| | Lineker |
| | Samways |
| | Nayim |

### LEAGUE POSITION

| P | W | D | L | F | A | Pts | Pos |
|---|---|---|---|---|---|-----|-----|
| 10 | 4 | 2 | 4 | 19 | 17 | 14 | 11th |

*Brian McClair puts the Reds back on the crest of a wave against Southampton.*

# RED DEVILS' DIARY: November

## Jekyll and Hyde form

By November it looked as though United were at last getting close to the kind of form expected of their big-name stars. The erratic start to the season had seen sensational victories and disastrous defeats and the search for consistency continued. Injuries had been Alex Ferguson's biggest problem; by the fourth month of the season he had used 21 different players in the 13 fixtures played – one player less than in the whole of the 1987–88 season.

Neil Webb was making progress but was still side-lined. He had set himself a target of being back in action by March and was confident that he would make it. His absence was an obvious blow for United and it shattered Fergie's plans to field the backbone of England's midfield in his side. Danny Wallace joined the injured shortly after his arrival when he pulled a hamstring and missed three games, but by the start of November he was ready for a comeback.

Russell Beardsmore and Viv Anderson were injured but Paul Ince, who had caused a scare when he limped off during the win over Southampton in the final game of October, looked like being fit for the next match. Other long-term injuries had raised doubts about the future of three former regulars in the squad: Colin Gibson had been on the verge of a comeback but had broken down again after surgery on his knee; goalkeeper Gary Walsh had been out of action for two seasons; and defender Billy Garton was still fighting his way back after a long absence.

Walsh had looked as though he had a bright future when, as a 19-year-old, he was part of Alex Ferguson's side that finished runners-up in 1987–88, but after he was badly concussed in an exciting game at Sheffield Wednesday, and then again a few weeks

> 'I think people expected Brian McClair and me to play well together straight away, but it does take time for a striking partnership to gel. We get on well enough, so there are no problems in that direction. It's funny how rumours start flying about that we don't speak to each other and such like, but that's a load of nonsense. We're good friends and the only time we have a bad word is when we're on the golf course. Clayton Blackmore and I always play Brian and Jim Leighton, the Scots against the Welsh, and as we're two up at the moment you can see what I mean!'
>
> **Mark Hughes**
> *3 November*

later during a friendly in Bermuda, he began to have problems. He was out for the remainder of that season and had only just recovered from that crisis when a stress fracture of his ankle forced him out of the side. There were more worries when surgery failed to find a cure.

Billy Garton had almost signed for Manchester City during the summer of 1988, but Alex Ferguson refused to release him only for back trouble to keep him out of the game. Then he was struck down by ME – 'yuppie' 'flu'.

## Saturday 4 November

Just when it seemed safe to go back in the water along came Charlton. After two successive League wins United returned to Selhurst Park, scene of their first away game of 1989–90. On that visit Crystal Palace had celebrated their return to the First Division with a firework display. This time it was a damp squib!

On the eve of Guy Fawkes' Night United faced homeless Charlton, who had shared the Crystal Palace Stadium since losing their own ground at the Valley. The Reds did enough to be four up by half time yet Charlton won 2–0.

United were trying to find a way through the

Charlton defence when Fergie decided to take a gamble. Mal Donaghy was pulled off and Clayton Blackmore took his place. Paul Ince was moved to right back with Blackmore in midfield. It didn't work. Within two minutes, as United apparently tried to adjust to the changes, Charlton struck twice, and it was uphill all the way from then.

Fergie was speechless after the game, but before the next fixture another manager had plenty to say. In a magazine article, Nottingham Forest boss Brian Clough claimed *he* should have been offered the United job in 1979 when Dave Sexton was sacked. His comments were far from welcome at Old Trafford, but Fergie had the last laugh . . .

*Gary Pallister powers in the ball from close range for the winning goal against Nottingham Forest.*

but Pally made doubly sure, powering it into the roof of the net from close range.

Before the game Fergie had been criticised for selecting Paul Ince to start at right back – he was a midfield expert, after all – but he looked competent and polished in that position, even though Ron Atkinson voted neither Pallister nor Ince as his ITV Man of the Match. Instead he chose a below average Bryan Robson – the only player on the field that he had bought during his days as United's boss!

> *'Anyone who has just moved house can get a good idea of how things are going here at the moment. When you move you try to put all your furniture and ornaments in the right place but they don't look right. They did in your old home but not in the new one, so you have to switch things about until it comes good. It's the same with new players who all fitted in well at their old clubs. Team unity is what we're looking for, sometimes we have looked very good, but other times we just frustrate ourselves and lose to terrible goals and we're left to face all the criticism you expect when you lose at this club. It's very difficult to put your finger on, it's just getting that consistency that will put things right.'*
>
> ### Alex Ferguson
> *7 November*

## Sunday 12 November

United appeared on live television for the first time in the season and the clash with Forest did enough to show the armchair critics that all was not lost at Old Trafford. The Reds were being dubbed Fergie's Failures in the tabloid press, but they turned on a thrilling display even though there was only one goal.

Many of the critics expected Forest to run riot, but United maintained the upper hand throughout and Cloughie sat tight-lipped on the trainers' bench listening to the taunts of the crowd.

Gary Pallister had his best game since that big-money transfer and topped the performance with his first goal in a United shirt. The 44th-minute strike was created by Steve Bruce, who got his head to a cross from the left. The ball looked as though it was going in,

> *'Brucie's a bit disappointed that I took the goal off him, but he did great to get up and put the ball across and I just made sure. It was great scoring my first goal, but I didn't think that I had anything to prove with all this talk about my big transfer fee – people can write what they like as far as I'm concerned, it's not for me to get involved with what they say. I was just delighted to score the goal today.'*
>
> ### Gary Pallister
> *12 November*

The win put United back in 11th spot. They had slipped two places after the Charlton defeat, and as far as the fans were concerned the only way now was up.

Throughout the season United had hardly been out of the news; new signings and poor results, speculation about the future of the manager, newspaper articles by former players casting a shadow over the club and all the take-over talk had kept the club constantly in the spotlight. The win over Forest seemed to calm things down – perhaps United would have a successful season after all?

Plans were being made for the club's annual meeting and it was obvious that the share-holders would have plenty to say about the happenings both on and off the field. The balance sheet showed that the club had made a healthy profit of almost £2 million, despite spending big money on Webb and Phelan. However, the buying of Pallister, Ince and Wallace in the new financial year had plunged United £4 million into the red, a clear illustration of why success on the field was vital.

## Saturday 18 November

Danny Wallace did his bit to balance the books with his first League goal early in the game against Luton, playing a major part in a 3–1 victory. The Kenilworth

Road plastic, feared by so many, had no adverse effect on a lively United who played at their best. Fast running, swift passing and accurate finishing made it a one-horse race.

Following that first goal, Clayton Blackmore blasted home a superb volley when Wallace picked out Brian McClair with a pass to the right wing, and then after Luton had pulled one back, Mark Hughes put matters beyond their reach. Again, Wallace was at the heart of the action, finding Hughes with a long ball from inside the centre circle, and Sparky made no mistake with his finishing shot.

The victory moved the Reds to ninth in the table, their highest position since the previous March. It also

*Paul Ince compliments Danny Wallace on his first League goal in United's 3–1 win over Luton.*

*Danny Wallace played a vital role in the 3–1 victory at Luton, which changed the pattern of results.*

*Jim Leighton, who recorded his fourth 'clean sheet' of the season against Chelsea.*

changed the pattern of results – for the first time in the season they had won two successive League games.

## Saturday 25 November

Frustration for Fergie and the fans. It seemed as though the missing supporters had started to return to the terraces as 47,106 paid to see high-flying Chelsea at Old Trafford. But it turned out to be a disappointing goal-less draw as United failed to penetrate a defence which was as packed as the terraces.

Chelsea had won promotion the previous season, but they gained few friends in a dull game. There were some anxious moments for both goalkeepers but scoring chances were minimal and the moaners who had returned to the terraces had a field day.

The crowd turned its wrath on the new players. Jeers greeted the exit of Luton hero Wallace, who was replaced by Russell Beardsmore, and the catcalls were coming from United supporters. Mike Duxbury, who took over from Lee Martin, was given similar treatment and it was obvious that patience was running out for some.

Only Jim Leighton could salvage any consolation from the result. It gave him his fourth 'clean sheet' of the season, his third in the League, and even this was a shadow of the form shown by the Scotland 'keeper on his arrival the previous season when he'd had eight shut-outs in 11 games.

Inconsistency was costing United valuable points and the Jekyll and Hyde form seemed to be affecting the confidence of the players. Brian McClair had scored just four times in 17 games, half the total netted by Mark Hughes, and those Championship hopes were looking bleak.

### NOVEMBER RESULTS

| | |
|---|---|
| *Charlton Atheltic 2* | *Manchester United 0* |
| Williams (2) | |
| *Manchester United 1* | *Nottingham Forest 0* |
| Pallister | |
| *Luton 1* | *Manchester United 3* |
| Wilson | Wallace |
| | Blackmore |
| | Hughes |
| *Manchester United 0* | *Chelsea 0* |

### LEAGUE POSITION

| P | W | D | L | F | A | Pts | Pos |
|---|---|---|---|---|---|---|---|
| 14 | 6 | 3 | 5 | 23 | 20 | 21 | 10th |

# NEIL'S TARGET FOR SUCCESS

Neil Webb's move to United after a highly successful spell with Nottingham Forest hit the headlines in the summer of 1989, but just a month into the season he was making news for a very different reason. After only four games his career hung in the balance. The England midfielder had so much to look forward to when he signed for the Reds, but suddenly all those hopes were dashed one night in Sweden.

'I remember it quite clearly,' says Neil, 'although there isn't a lot to remember! I think the ball had rebounded off a defender and I was going after it when I felt my ankle give way under me. I fell over and there was very little feeling in my leg. It felt quite dead. I knew straight away that something serious had happened and the England physio got me off the field quickly. Before I knew it I was back home and on my way to the operating theatre!'

Neil had ruptured his Achilles' tendon, and although it was then only early September, United were told that he would be lucky to play again during the 1989–90 season. It was a blow for the Reds and for their new player.

'I realised then that it was going to be hard to get back, but I had no intention of just sitting there and doing nothing, so I set myself targets throughout the months which followed – little things like aiming to be jogging by a certain date, then building up to light running then, as I grew stronger, running normally. I was looking forward to kicking a ball again, and eventually I reached that target. Looking ahead gave me the incentive to get fit quickly.

As his strength came back Neil realised that he perhaps had a chance of returning to the side for the last few games of the season. It was only an outside chance, but it was better than nothing. 'If I'd been told that it would be impossible to play again before the 1990–91 season then I might well have thought about packing my bags and heading off on holiday somewhere. I'd have told everybody that I'd see them in time for pre-season training and left it at that. But when the specialist said I would probably play again before May, that became the ultimate target.'

The seven months out of action were the bleakest spell of a career which began in his home town of

*The fateful night in Sweden that heralded the bleakest spell of Neil Webb's career.*

*'There can be nothing worse for a footballer than to be out of the game for a long period', says Neil.*

Reading before Neil was transferred to Nottingham Forest. 'It was a nightmare. I had joined United with high hopes of achieving something with the biggest club in the country, and suddenly I couldn't play.

'Things had been so promising when I moved to Old Trafford. The Gaffer was building his side and I felt very much an integral part of his plans. We got off to a great start, and I was thrilled to bits to score on my debut. Then, three games later, disaster.'

As the months went by the reluctant spectator watched United's struggle in the League, and followed his team-mates' progress in the FA Cup. 'I was delighted to go to Nottingham in January and to see the lads do well. That gave me quite a boost.'

By February he was given the news he had been waiting for. 'I was told I might be able to play football again within a month. It was the best news I had heard in months', he says. 'There is nothing worse for a footballer than to be out of the game for a long period. You begin to worry that you might not get back at all, and at first, when I began my build-up, I thought about the injury all the time. When I trained alone I couldn't take my mind off it. Every time I stepped up my programme I wondered if there would be any pain. But then I began running with Bryan Robson, who was also out of action, and because I had someone to talk to my mind was on other things, and I never gave the ankle a thought.'

It was the same when Neil eventually rejoined his colleagues for full training sessions: 'You wonder how you will react, but then you become wrapped up in what is going on and realise that you have gone through a full session without any problems'.

So came the big day. After having been out since 6 September, Neil saw his name on the team sheet – for a Reserve game on 17 March. Neil Webb was back! At the time United were in deep trouble, fighting against

relegation. A week after his come-back Neil was plunged into the thick of things.

The Reds were away to Southampton and desperate for points. Neil was on the team coach as a player for the first time since he'd travelled to Derby on 26 August. 'It was a great feeling, joining in with training, the laughs with the lads, being part of it all again. You don't realise how much you have missed.'

So, on Saturday 24 March, months of anguish ended when he ran on as substitute to help in a 2–0 win – a small step for Neil Webb and a giant stride towards safety for United.

The struggle to get back into the game was over now, and Neil had other targets. 'When I was recovering from the operation people talked about me returning by the end of the season. By that I imagined a couple of games around the last days of April or early May. I would have been quite happy to settle for that at one stage. However, when we reached the semi-final of the FA Cup the target was obvious: to get to Wembley, and to be back in the England squad in time to make it to the World Cup in Italy.'

And make it he did. 'Reaching the FA Cup final was tremendous. And while I wasn't happy with my performance in the first game, the replay made up for all the frustration of being out of action for months. If someone had told me when I was lying in hospital that I would play in the winning side in the 1990 FA Cup final, I would have thought they were kidding.'

Not only did Neil play, but his skill also provided the pass for the winning goal, and his performance guaranteed his inclusion in the England World Cup squad. Neil Webb was back.

*The chance of playing in the FA Cup final gave Neil the incentive he needed to overcome his injury within the season.*

# RED DEVILS' DIARY: December

## A rough ride for chairman Edwards

United approached the end of the 1980s with a performance record bettered only by Liverpool – but that Championship trophy had failed to find its way to Old Trafford for yet another decade.

United's average position for the period was 5.2, a figure based on the outcome of ten seasons from 1979–80, when they finished runners-up under Dave Sexton's management, to 1988–89, when they were 11th. In Alex Ferguson's first full season they had taken second place, but the Scot also suffered the ignominy of his side finishing outside the top ten in 1986–87: two out of three seasons in 11th place.

Alex knew when he took over the manager's role that life at Old Trafford would not be easy and success

> 'I don't think it is pleasant when you are sitting up there on a top table in front of share-holders and they call for your resignation. I'm disappointed. It's difficult to know what more I can do as chairman; I have sanctioned the spending in ten years of £21 million, and when you've spent £7 million since the end of last season and people still call for your resignation it's a shattering blow. I've got a lot of thinking to do and this is not the time to make a quick decision.'
>
> *Martin Edwards*
> 5 December

would be measured only by League achievement. Before him Ron Atkinson, Dave Sexton, Tommy Docherty, Frank O'Farrell and Wilf McGuinness shared some glory, but none had been able to match the achievements of Sir Matt Busby, who led the club to five League titles.

So, as the last month of the year began with a trip to Arsenal and United sat halfway up the First Division, there were still rumblings of discontent among certain factions. Alex Ferguson was being judged solely on the performance of the first team; anything he had done to improve the club at other levels meant little to his critics.

### Sunday 3 December

United faced the reigning champions, Arsenal, for a second time, but the encounter was nothing like the first. Sunshine and five goals made the August game memorable, mist and missed chances made the return fixture anything but!

Most of the misses were Arsenal's as United lost their way and offered little challenge to the Gunners. To make matters worse, the game was televised and United were really put under the microscope by their armchair audience – at least by those who managed to stay awake.

It seemed as if their only hope was that the fog which hung around Highbury would descend and bring about an early finish, but it didn't and it became clear that United still had problems. However if that result was bad, two days later things seemed even worse . . .

### Tuesday 5 December

The biggest attendance in the club's history for the Annual General Meeting called for chairman Martin Edwards to resign and to take Michael Knighton with him! The publicity which had surrounded the abortive

## Saturday 9 December

Four days after the AGM Fergie came under fire. United slumped 1–2 to Crystal Palace, and he tried a brave experiment only to have it explode in his face. He played Brian McClair as his main striker along with Danny Wallace, and dropped Mark Hughes to substitute. Brave, or crazy?

Evidence showed that without Hughes McClair had scored 31 goals in his first season, yet he had managed only 17 the following term after he was joined by the Welshman. McClair had scored just four goals by the start of December, and Hughes eight. Was he dropping the right man? It was a calculated gamble but it failed.

McClair certainly looked sharp enough and went close to scoring on a couple of occasions, and he was involved when Russell Beardsmore headed home a brilliant goal in the ninth minute to boost hopes. But as Palace got back into the game the popularity of Hughes began to outweigh the patience of the supporters. For the first time 'Fergie Out!' was the cry from parts of the ground, and it was coming from United supporters not from impish visitors.

The result provided more ammunition for those critics who appeared to take delight in attacking the club. Throughout the season there had been predictions on some back pages that it would not be long before Alex lost his job and this led to unsettling speculation as to who would take over. Some of the

take-over had proved too much for the share-holders. The angry meeting even refused to vote Knighton on to the board, and only the majority holding of chairman Edwards secured his seat.

It was another chance for the knockers to go to work, but Alex Ferguson cleverly side-stepped what could have been an embarrassing public questioning when he told the share-holders that he would answer any of their queries after the meeting, and away from the ears of the media.

The United manager then stood for well over an hour surrounded by a large group of supporters, answering each and every one of their questions. Satisfied with his replies, they left the gathering in a happier mood.

*Russell Beardsmore heads home a spectacular goal, but it wasn't enough to prevent defeat against Crystal Palace.*

writers had been stunned and a little embarrassed when Manchester City appointed their new manager a few days before the Palace game – Howard Kendall, tipped by many to be the next at United, had returned from Spain to take over the job at Maine Road.

## Saturday 16 December

On the day United faced Tottenham Hotspur at Old Trafford there came another sensation when directors Bobby Charlton and Amer Midani broke their silence about the future of the club. From the start of the Knighton saga, United's board had agreed that the chairman would act as their only spokesman. The other directors remained tight-lipped despite the varying speculation and the weekly naming of potential buyers in the press.

*Controversy at board level continued in December, prompting Bobby Charlton to silence newspaper rumours.*

The reaction of the supporters at the Annual General Meeting and a newspaper story which claimed that Bobby Charlton would be the next chairman if one particular group of businessmen bought the club brought the unexpected statements.

> *'I don't like being taken for granted and having people putting my name forward as chairman if they take over the club. I don't want to be chairman of Manchester United, it's not my turn, I don't really think that I'm qualified, and I don't really like being used as a pawn in the game.'*
>
> ## Bobby Charlton
> 16 December

> *'My exercise to buy Manchester United, especially after the recent events, was really to float it back. Because I do believe wholeheartedly that it should be owned by the people. It belongs to the people, it's an institution, and it should never belong to an individual, and I know these are thoughts shared by some of the other directors.'*
>
> ## Amer Midani
> 16 December

Bobby Charlton made a public announcement that he objected to his name being used by anyone without his permission, and said he had no ambitions to be chairman. Amer Midani joined in and said that he felt that Martin Edwards should offer his shares to the public, that United should be 'floated' on the stock market, and that no one man should ever again have control. All this won support from the terraces, but the result that afternoon was another disappointment.

Spurs won 1–0, and hit a post and the crossbar, while United had two goals and two penalty appeals turned down. The Reds slumped to 13th in the table. Was this going to be an unlucky Christmas for Fergie?

## Saturday 23 December

Because of the behaviour of the crowd towards him at the Crystal Palace game, the manager described it as 'the worst day of my life', yet two days before Christmas his frustrating players came close to giving him his best-ever present. They showed how unpredictable they were by totally outplaying Liverpool at Anfield.

The game had sparked off a row between ITV and the Football League. First, it had been switched from earlier in the season to accommodate television, then, because of safety problems, the police had insisted that it be moved from the re-scheduled Friday night to Saturday lunch-time. Finally, by using delayed transmission, the first half was screened while the second was still being played, which meant a smaller fee for the clubs because the game was not 'live'. The League hierarchy were far from happy. As for the United fans, they were delirious. United were unlucky not to score six!

United ran Liverpool off the park and earned all the praise heaped upon them by the same critics who had been after their heads a few days earlier. It was the 20th First Division clash of the 1980s between the two

A delighted Mark Robins celebrates his goal against Wimbledon. Alas, the Reds had to be content with a draw.

giants, and although it ended goal-less it gave United a remarkable record against Liverpool.

Despite Liverpool's overall success during the decade, the tally of the annual clashes between Manchester and Merseyside stood at eight wins to United and just two to the Anfield club. Beating Liverpool 8–2 is no mean achievement!

## Tuesday 26 December

If Santa arrived early at Liverpool, he came back down the chimney on Boxing Day and stole United's presents. Aston Villa had avoided relegation by a whisker the previous season, but there were no signs of that when the Reds played their post-Christmas game at Villa Park.

It was another early kick-off and United played as though they could have done with an extra hour in bed. There were no goals by half-time, which gave some hope to the thousands who had made the trip down the M6 motorway that morning. Villa had other ideas, however, and stepped up a gear, scoring three times in just over 20 minutes to spoil the party.

The defeat made it six games without a win and with a trip to Wimbledon coming next the chances of that record reaching seven seemed likely. United had never won a game at Plough Lane.

## Saturday 30 December

The United manager decided on another formula in his quest for goals and success – and this time it paid off. He played Mark Robins up front with Mark Hughes and pulled Brian McClair back into midfield. Robins went into the game with a remarkable scoring record. Twice he had scored more than 50 goals in a season with the junior sides but had yet to taste success at senior level.

Wimbledon's style of play made life difficult for United in general and for Jim Leighton in particular, and it was no surprise when central defender Eric Young gave them a first-half lead. In the second it was

a different story as United took control.

After a string of chances Mark Hughes got his ninth of the season with a shot from a Steve Bruce header; then Mark Robins found his way into the record books. Two minutes after the Hughes goal he got his head to a cross from the Welsh striker to score.

The travelling supporters celebrated, but just when it seemed that United would end their run with an away victory, Wimbledon snatched a last-kick equaliser.

So the decade closed with the Reds 15th in the table. The dream of the Championship looked as though it would have to wait for another year – only the optimists could see success coming in the FA Cup.

## DECEMBER RESULTS

| | |
|---|---|
| Arsenal 1 | Manchester United 0 |
| Groves | |
| | |
| Manchester United 1 | Crystal Palace 2 |
| Beardsmore | Bright (2) |
| | |
| Manchester United 0 | Tottenham Hotspur 1 |
| | Lineker |
| | |
| Liverpool 0 | Manchester United 0 |
| | |
| Aston Villa 3 | Manchester United 0 |
| Olney | |
| Platt | |
| Gage | |
| | |
| Wimbledon 2 | Manchester United 2 |
| Young | Hughes |
| Cork | Robins |

### LEAGUE POSITION

| P | W | D | L | F | A | Pts | Pos |
|---|---|---|---|---|---|---|---|
| 20 | 6 | 5 | 9 | 26 | 29 | 23 | 15th |

# *RED DEVILS' DIARY:*
## *January*

## *Forest foiled by Red Red Robins*

With half of the season gone it was obvious that United had to improve or there would be serious consequences. They were 15th in the table, too far away from the top to pose a serious threat to the leaders, but close enough to the bottom to feel the magnetic pull of relegation. It was hard to believe that one of the teams tipped before the 1989–90 season to take the title was now a possible contender for one of the First Division's three unwanted places.

The New Year started with high hopes rather than high spirits. The players ended 1989 by spending a quiet night in a city centre hotel, away from New Year's Eve revellers, and they were in a relaxed mood when they travelled by coach to Old Trafford the next morning. The promise shown at Liverpool and Wimbledon had lifted the hopes of some supporters, but the first game of 1990 brought back all the old frustrations.

### *Monday 1 January*

Queen's Park Rangers used their sweeper system to good effect, blocking out anything United could produce. The Reds did create chances, but that final touch was still missing and the match resulted in another 0–0 draw. A crowd of only 34,824 turned up, good by some standards but only just above United's break-even figure. The poor attendance showed that some fans were voting with their feet. Only two League games had attracted lower crowds at Old Trafford since the start of the season.

> ### *Captain Fantastic OBE!*
>
> *Bryan Robson's achievements on the football field were rewarded when the United and England skipper was named in the New Year's Honours list, receiving an OBE for services to the game.*
> *'I think it's smashing, and what a pick-me-up it's been for everyone at the club! It means that Manchester United are making the headlines for a different reason than of late.*
> *'It's great for Bryan and his family and I think his folks in the north-east will be so proud of him. We're proud of him too, and it's a great boost for the club.*
> *'Goodness knows what would have happened if we had won the League in the last few years – probably all the players would have got an award!'*
>
> ### *Alex Ferguson*

Rangers paraded their latest signing, a familiar figure to United's followers – Ray Wilkins, the former Reds skipper, who had been sold to Italian giants AC Milan in 1984 after failing to fit into Ron Atkinson's plans. His travels had then taken him to Paris St Germain and Glasgow Rangers. Ray controlled much of the midfield battle and almost scored against his old club – a rarity in the Wilkins repertoire!

There was a certain irony as the obviously very fit ex-England star showed he had lost none of his skills, but the man who had replaced him as captain of both club and country, his close friend Bryan Robson, was out injured. Did Atkinson sell Wilkins too soon? Would he and Robson have established a formidable midfield? But Robbo wasn't fit for the reunion, and the news that he had failed to recover from a slight groin strain was later to prove ominous. The United star had played the whole of the Liverpool game eight days earlier despite the injury, picked up in training. He missed the games at Villa and Wimbledon, but had been expected to make New Year's Day.

United seemed to have gone ahead in the 25th minute, but a Mark Robins strike was ruled offside, and just before the end the fair-haired youngster missed from close range.

So the bad form continued – eight games without a League win, and just three goals since 18 November. Could the FA Cup provide United with the springboard to success?

## Sunday 7 January

Thousands of supporters made the trip to Nottingham for the third round Cup tie against a Forest side that had hit a great streak of form since losing to United at Old Trafford. Brian Clough's side were firm favourites to win, but United surprised everyone, especially their television critics. Before the 'live' game Jimmy Hill told viewers that he felt Forest would win easily because United showed no enthusiasm – and that was during the kick-about! Fergie's team, unaware of the comment, had other ideas, however.

The injury crisis had hit hard. Bryan Robson was out for the fourth successive game, and Danny Wallace and Paul Ince joined him.

United won 1–0 and Mark Robins was the hero again, scoring with a well-placed header from a Mark Hughes cross. It was nothing more than United deserved after dominating play for long periods, but there was a nail-biting finish which brought back memories of the 1989 quarter-final clash, when United were knocked out by a lone Forest goal after what they thought was an equaliser was ruled out by the referee because he felt the ball had not crossed the line.

*Mark Robins battles against Nottingham Forest's Des Walker and Brian Laws.*

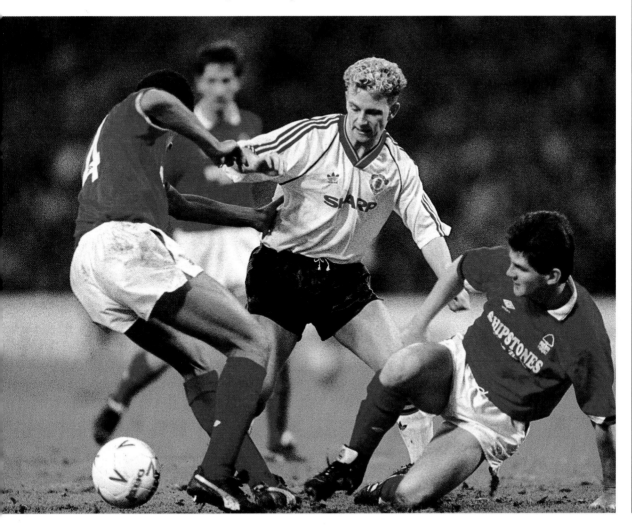

This time it was Forest's turn. They threw players forward in a last-ditch attempt to equalise, and minutes before the end got the ball into the net only for the strike to be disallowed. Television showed clearly that not only had Jim Leighton been fouled, but a Forest player was offside. The referee had no hesitation in ruling out the goal.

## Saturday 13 January

With a place in the fourth round of the FA Cup secured United had to concentrate on lifting themselves away from the lower reaches of the League table, but what a shock they got when Derby County came to Old Trafford. That day the Football League had issued a directive to referees to toughen up, and Darlington official Robert Hart did just that.

Two players were sent off and five booked as United went down 2–1 in front of a crowd of 38,985. Steve Bruce was first to go, for a trip on Dean Saunders, and United had to play 80 minutes without him. Hindmarch, Rammage, Phelan and Blackmore were booked and then, eight minutes from time, Derby's Mark Wright was cautioned for a second time and given his marching orders.

To the United fans the bookings meant little but the result did. The Reds were 19 points away from the top, but only two above the relegation zone.

## Sunday 21 January

Norwich City always seem to be a 'bogey' team to the Reds, and a Sunday visit to Carrow Road brought more gloom for Fergie. The newspapers were

'United seem to be lacking just that little bit of confidence and belief to go and play. They obviously have the talent, they've got some super players, but it's just a question of them getting that belief in themselves. When they bring their game together they look a terrific team.'

*Ray Wilkins*

speculating that the United boss would have been out of a job if his players had been knocked out of the Cup at Forest, and the predictions continued as their League form dropped.

The fixture had the sportswriters reaching for their record books to see when United had last gone ten games without a League win, and the headlines were already written before the kick-off.

Norwich won 2–0. United were 17th.

The Reds never looked like getting anything out of the game and created only a couple of scoring chances, leaving Alex Ferguson a bewildered man.

It was in the early '70s, in the days of Frank O'Farrell that the Reds had last experienced such a dismal run, although during 1973–74, the relegation season, under Tommy Docherty their overall performances had been worse.

## Sunday 28 January

Doom and gloom forgotten for a moment, United went to Hereford to face a club that held a great reputation for giant-killing in the FA Cup. Would

LEFT: *Steve Bruce was the first to feel the effects of a refereeing clampdown in the game against Derby County.*

RIGHT: *Clayton Blackmore destroyed Hereford's giant-killing hopes in the fourth round of the FA Cup.*

mighty Manchester United be another scalp?

The weather played its part. Herefordshire was under water, or so it seemed to the 6,000 United fans who journeyed south. The pitch was like a sponge pudding, and when Hereford paraded their traditional live bull around the ground before the kick-off, he sank into the mud leaving a trail of footprints like craters.

Everything was ready for a Cup upset.

The game had been moved to a Sunday at the request of the local police and the Edgar Street ground was packed. Hereford never really lived up to their reputation, and while it took a late goal from Clayton Blackmore to get United through, Jim

Leighton had only one anxious moment. That came when someone in the crowd blew a whistle and United's defence stopped playing. Leighton carried on and saved bravely at the feet of Colin Robinson – not once but twice. It would have been rough justice if a goal had been scored.

So the month came to an end with United through to the fifth round of the FA Cup, yet still at the wrong end of the League table. Neil Webb was progressing towards his comeback target, but there were dark clouds looming for Bryan Robson.

## JANUARY RESULTS

| | |
|---|---|
| *Manchester United 0* | *Queen's Park Rangers 0* |

| | |
|---|---|
| *Manchester United 1* | *Derby County 2* |
| Pallister | Wright |
| | Pickering |

| | |
|---|---|
| *Norwich City 2* | *Manchester United 0* |
| Fleck (2) | |

### FA CUP
#### ROUND 3

| | |
|---|---|
| *Nottingham Forest 0* | *Manchester United 1* |
| | Robins |

#### ROUND 4

| | |
|---|---|
| *Hereford 0* | *Manchester United 1* |
| | Blackmore |

### LEAGUE POSITION

| P | W | D | L | F | A | Pts | Pos |
|---|---|---|---|---|---|-----|-----|
| 23 | 6 | 6 | 11 | 27 | 33 | 24 | 17th |

# UNITED TAKE THE TOUGH ROUTE TO CUP GLORY

Without doubt the 1990 road to Wembley was the toughest in United's history. For the first time they were drawn away from home in every single round, and even when it came to the semi-finals the Reds' number came out of the bag behind that of opponents Oldham Athletic!

The record books show that United have had some pretty tough passages to the final, and older supporters were quick to point out to the modern-day statisticians that when the 1948 side won the Cup they did so without playing a single game at Old Trafford. True – but there is a twist to that tale: United *were* drawn at home for three of their ties in the 1947–48 season, but because Old Trafford had been damaged by wartime bombing and was still under repair, they played their 'home' games on neutral grounds. In fact at that time they were using Maine Road as their base, sharing the stadium with rivals Manchester City, but as the Blues were involved in the Cup themselves in the early rounds United had to borrow other grounds.

Drawn away in the third round they beat Aston Villa 6–4 and began their nomadic route to Wembley. In the next round they were drawn at 'home' to Liverpool, but played the tie at Goodison Park. That proved too much for the Merseysiders, who were beaten 3–0. Next came a game at Leeds Road, home of Huddersfield Town, against Charlton Athletic, and a 2–0 win saw United through to the sixth round.

Again their name came out first as they were paired with Preston North End, and as Maine Road was available for the tie on 28 February 1948 it was the nearest they came to playing at home that season. Victory over Preston saw them into the semi-finals, where they beat Derby County 3–1 at Hillsborough, and then it was a trip to Wembley for the first time.

United had played in the FA Cup final just once before, in 1909, before the famous Empire Stadium was built. That final was played at Crystal Palace. So 1948 saw the start of regular visits to the twin towers as they beat Blackpool 4–2 in a memorable final. It

*It was Destination Wembley for Manchester United in 1990!*

seems amazing that there should be a gap of 39 years between Cup successes: in that time they only reached the semi-finals once, in 1926, when they lost to Manchester City at Bramall Lane.

As it turned out Bramall Lane became one of the milestones along the 1990 route to the final, a road which was uphill all the way for the Reds. The 1989 campaign had ended at Old Trafford when Nottingham Forest beat United in the quarter-finals, and in 1990 the clubs had to face each other again in the third round. Only the most fervent Red felt that United had much chance of progressing further in the competition – away to Nottingham Forest, when Brian Clough's side were enjoying a run of success and United were on the crest of a slump!

Plagued by injuries, and with eight games without a win behind them, United lined up: Leighton, Anderson, Martin, Bruce, Phelan, Pallister, Beardsmore, Blackmore, McClair, Hughes, Robins. Mike Duxbury and Ralph Milne were the substitutes. Without Robson, Ince or Wallace, and with Neil Webb in the middle of a long lay-off, United were down to the bare bones, but they pulled off a great win.

Mark Robins scored the only goal to steal the headlines for the first – but certainly not the last – time. 'It was a wonderful feeling getting my first FA Cup goal,' he said afterwards, 'but Mark Hughes made it so easy for me. All I had to do was stick out my head, the ball was there and in it went.'

Modest Mark was perhaps understating his performance, but he had shown millions of armchair football fans watching the Sunday tie on television that he was a cool-headed finisher under pressure, and they would soon find out that there was more to come!

In the next round United were drawn away to Hereford, one-time giant-killers who fancied their chances against the struggling Reds. League form was hard to explain and the critics were tipping United for relegation, but the fans felt there was hope in the Cup. The run had started at Nottingham and it continued in

*Peacock of Hereford tangles with Mark Hughes. United put paid to the home side's giant-killing hopes.*

the mud of Edgar Street when a close-range Clayton Blackmore shot took the Reds through.

The team that day was: Leighton, Anderson, Martin, Donaghy, Duxbury, Pallister, Blackmore, Ince, McClair, Hughes, Wallace. Russell Beardsmore and Mark Robins were the substitutes.

This time Mark stayed on the bench, but he was in the thick of things in the next round. 'I've got that feeling that our name's on the Cup,' said United director Bobby Charlton when he heard the draw for the fifth round, 'but it'll be tough at St James's Park.' The Magpies of Newcastle have a great tradition of Cup glory, and their supporters wanted to taste success again. Being drawn against United created the perfect recipe for a tremendous Cup tie.

Steve Bruce, who had been suspended for the Hereford game, was back again to play against the club he had supported as a boy. 'When I was a little lad I used to watch Newcastle and I always felt that one day I'd like to play for them – every Geordie boy does. But that was before Manchester United, of course – now I wouldn't want to change anything', said Steve before the clash.

As for Mark Robins, he had achieved his ambition to play for the side he had supported and which his policeman father has always followed, and it was Cup goal number two for the young striker that started the thrills that afternoon. Nineteen minutes had gone when United had a corner on the left. Danny Wallace floated the ball over and there was Robins on the far post, leaping up to head home a sweet goal.

*Cup goal number two for Mark Robins came in spectacular style against Newcastle.*

*With the 3–2 win over Newcastle under his belt, Alex Ferguson monitors United's performance at Bramall Lane in the sixth round.*

Newcastle fought back, and after Steve Bruce had brought down Mark McGhee they levelled the score from the penalty spot in the 50th minute. But Geordie joy was short-lived as United went ahead again on the hour when Danny Wallace hit a beauty, ramming the ball into the roof of the net from an acute angle.

'It was a goal that gave me a great deal of pleasure. I was thrilled to join United and all I wanted to do was to pay back the supporters for the way they get behind us', said Danny. 'The atmosphere at Newcastle was amazing, and we all felt when we won that game that we had a chance of getting to Wembley', he added.

The tie was far from over after the Wallace goal: the home fans urged Newcastle back into the game and, with 25 minutes to go, they scored a controversial equaliser. Jim Leighton was tripped as he came out to catch a cross from a corner on the Newcastle right. Referee Danny Vickers missed the incident, and Kevin Scott headed home. 'It was the sort of thing which could've turned the game,' said Fergie afterwards, 'but we kept going at them.'

Go at them United did, and 12 minutes from the end Brian McClair ended a personal goal drought. 'Danny gave me the perfect pass and it was a delight to see it going in', said Brian of his first goal in 18 games.

The line-up that afternoon was: Leighton, Anderson, Martin, Bruce, Phelan, Pallister, Robins, Duxbury, McClair, Hughes, Wallace. The substitutes were Paul Ince and Russell Beardsmore.

The victory meant a great deal to Alex Ferguson. 'I was told when I came to Old Trafford that United supporters would rather see their side lose a game 4–3 than win a dull game 1–0. I wondered what they meant, but now I know. The best way to beat somebody who scores three goals against you is to get four. Newcastle got two, so we got three!'

And Fergie's hopes for the next round? 'I don't care who we play as long as it's at home', he said. But you can't win them all – United were drawn away again, this time to Sheffield United, like Newcastle a Second Division side, but also up at the top of the table and hoping for promotion.

The Blades were managed by Dave 'Harry' Bassett, the former boss of Wimbledon and a thorn in United's side during his days at Plough Lane. Would Harry's up-and-under style of football outfox United and end their Cup ambitions?

Sunday 11 March saw United crossing the Pennines to face a Bramall Lane crowd of 30,000 Yorkshire voices and only 6,000 Reds fans. United's share of the ticket allocation had been reduced on safety grounds. It mattered not. United's followers had the most to cheer, and after a hectic opening the Reds began to dominate the game, restricting Sheffield to a few hopeful attacks.

The game was in complete contrast to the New-castle tie. There was just one goal, and that was hotly disputed by the home supporters. It came in the 29th minute. Mark Robins chased a loose ball towards the goal-line. He caught it just before it crossed, although television evidence showed that he only just made it. A Sheffield player challenged and United won a corner. Over came the cross, Brian McClair got his head to it and Simon Tracey, the Blades' 'keeper, palmed the ball on to the crossbar. As it dropped, McClair prodded home the only goal of the game. 'It may have looked from off the field as though we were totally on top for most of the game, but Sheffield were always a threat,' said Brian, 'and I can tell you I was quite pleased to see that goal go in.'

The United line-up was: Leighton, Anderson, Martin, Bruce, Phelan, Pallister, Robins, Ince, McClair, Hughes, Wallace. The substitutes were Mike Duxbury (who replaced Viv Anderson at half-time) and Russell Beardsmore.

United were in the semi-finals, drawn against Oldham Athletic, the Cup kings of the north-west. Oldham were already through to Wembley in the Littlewoods Cup, and the Reds' clash with them is worth a story of its own!

*The ever-threatening Blades pursue Steve Bruce as he controls the ball.*

# RED DEVILS' DIARY: February

## Awayday Reds stay on the Cup trail

After victory over Hereford in the FA Cup United drove home through the flooded countryside to learn that they had another difficult journey in front of them in the fifth round. They were drawn away to Newcastle United, which made February an even tougher month than it had already seemed when the fixtures were first published.

United had just one home game to try to end their run of League matches without success, and that was against rivals Manchester City. Newspapers and television had no hesitation in recalling the horrors of 23 September in the build-up to the second derby of the season. For a week there were stories of the taunts endured by United supporters since 'Black Saturday', and City's five goals were played and replayed on radio and television.

Two successive League defeats had plunged United into trouble and City, under new manager Howard Kendall, were showing signs of a revival. They had risen from the bottom of the table to 14th – three places above the Reds. Criticism of Alex Ferguson's selections and United's performances continued, but the fact that they were still in the FA Cup had done a lot to boost a steadily sagging morale.

The United manager had plenty of sympathisers, too, and many people knew that a victory over City would be a tremendous confidence-booster.

> 'The media have had a field day speculating about my position, and I sometimes wonder whether they are more interested in a headline-hitting story than a true analysis of the situation.
>
> 'I don't squeal about criticism and I know it comes hot and strong at a club like Manchester United if things are not going right. I can take that – I expect it – but I must say that I am staggered by the non-stop sniping I am getting from Tommy Docherty, Pat Crerand and Willie Morgan. [on the radio and in newspaper articles.]
>
> 'They should have a better understanding of the problems and I would have thought that they would have more respect for the club they are supposed to care for than to undermine our work.'
>
> *Alex Ferguson*
> United v City match programme

## Saturday 3 February

Both teams were without key players as a crowd of 40,274 turned up to watch the 100th First Division clash between the two Manchester clubs. Steve Bruce was in the middle of a three-match ban after he was sent off against Derby County, and Bryan Robson was still not back in action. For City, £1 million striker

> 'I think it's the most frustrated I've been for ages, to know that there's been a lot of injuries in the squad, and I was perfectly fit and had to sit there for weeks because I was suspended. I just won't have to be as reckless in future, and maybe I've learned my lesson. I've served my punishment for being sent off and don't intend to do that again in a hurry.'
>
> *Steve Bruce*

Clive Allen was injured and player-coach Peter Reid, like Bruce, was serving a ban.

The game started at a hectic pace as United made most of the early running. They might have taken the lead when a four-man move put Mark Hughes through, but he shot wide. Brian McClair had a good scoring chance and Mike Phelan miscued in front of goal from a corner.

It looked good for United, but in the tenth minute

*Clayton Blackmore scores from a Wallace cross against rivals Manchester City.*

things suddenly fell apart and City were unlucky not to score. Gary Pallister, facing his own goal, tried a back pass to Jim Leighton but instead played the ball straight into the path of City striker Wayne Clarke. For a moment there was chaos in the United penalty area. Leighton saved bravely by throwing himself at the feet of Clarke, but as Mal Donaghy joined in the scramble he collapsed to the ground in agony.

The danger was cleared but the area looked like a battlefield as Leighton and Donaghy lay injured. Leighton quickly recovered but Donaghy, who had only just re-established himself in the side after he was temporarily loaned to his former club Luton, limped off. The Northern Ireland international had torn a hamstring and United had to re-jig their formation, bringing Russell Beardsmore off the bench.

That moment of madness seemed to affect United's confidence, and they fell apart as City created most of the chances before half-time. It was anything but a spectacle, the tension perhaps taking away any spark the fans had hoped for. Then, as the match went into its last quarter, there was a sudden change in tempo.

McClair found Wallace and he crossed a low, hard drive into the City penalty area. Clayton Blackmore ran in and threw himself at the ball, and the Stretford End erupted as United went in front. Was that Maine Road massacre to be avenged?

City had other ideas, and three minutes later converted one of their many chances. Ian Brightwell, the player who had been picked only because Reid was suspended, unleashed a super shot from the right-hand side of the field. The ball curled past Jim Leighton, who managed to touch it with the tips of his fingers as it flew into the net for a spectacular equaliser.

The goal earned City a point and added to United's woe – that unwanted record now stood at 11 games without a League win.

Before the next game came another blow. Bryan Robson went to see a Harley Street specialist in an effort to solve the problem that had kept him out since Christmas, and it was decided that surgery was the only answer. The skipper had a tear in a groin muscle and United were told that they would be without him for at least six weeks as he recovered from the operation.

No Robson, no Webb – Alex Ferguson's dream machine was off the road!

## Saturday 10 February

United were away to Millwall, one of the clubs struggling below them in the League, and the Reds knew that a lot was at stake on that damp afternoon at Cold Blow Lane. A win for Millwall would suck United into the bottom three, a position that was almost as bad as their plight in 1986 when Alex Ferguson had replaced Ron Atkinson. At that time they were 21st in a 22-team First Division, but under their new manager they climbed to 11th by the end of the season.

As they travelled to The Den, the United players only had to look at the back pages of any of the newspapers scattered around the team coach to see the magnitude of the task ahead. Defeat, even a draw, would equal a 60-year-old club record of 12 First Division matches without a win. They had to beat Millwall if only to save face.

The 1990 crisis was not quite as bad as the run which established the original record. Then, in the 1930–31 season, United had lost their first 12 games and, not surprisingly, finished the season at the bottom of the table. Their performances in 1989–90 provided five draws during the bad spell and, unlike their predecessors, they had won two FA Cup matches, so perhaps there was some light at the end of the tunnel.

But 26 minutes into the Millwall game United were stunned. A weak, looping header from Darren Morgan fooled Jim Leighton and dropped under the crossbar as the United 'keeper grabbed fresh air. Millwall were ahead.

The second half brought a transformation. United came out fighting and Mark Hughes was inspirational as he led the attack with skill and power, forcing Millwall to defend as the Reds went all-out for an equaliser. It came in the 65th minute when Russell Beardsmore crossed, Hughes headed downwards and across goal, and the ball struck a post. As it came out Danny Wallace was there to blast it home from close range – 1–1!

United never looked back. Six minutes from time Wallace broke away, rounded the Millwall defence and found Hughes with his cross. It was Mark's first goal of the '90s. Those record books went back on the shelves – with a bit of luck for another 60 years.

## Sunday 18 February

Only three of the fifth-round ties reached a conclusion the previous day as United prepared to take on Newcastle United in their televised Sunday Cup clash. Liverpool, Aston Villa and Steve Coppell's Crystal Palace were through, and the rest went to replays. Many felt that United's best result at St James's Park would be a draw.

The Reds took a big following to Tyneside, but they were drowned in a sea of noise from the Geordie supporters, who obviously thought that their side was in with more than a shout. Steve Bruce was back for United against the club he supported as a boy. It was a nostalgic return for the central defender, but there was a twist to the tale.

He revealed that he had never been on the winning side at Newcastle in his days with Norwich or since his transfer to Old Trafford – and that made anything but encouraging pre-match reading for United supporters!

Second Division Newcastle were slight favourites to pull off a surprise win, but as their confidence began to return United showed no signs of strain and took an early grip on the game. Brian McClair went wide with a diving header and Danny Wallace made some good runs. There were a few forays from Newcastle but the Reds' defence looked solid.

Then, in the 19th minute, United won a corner on the left. The cross came over and Mark Robins, on the far post, headed in. Although Newcastle scrambled the ball away the referee, standing on the goal-line

*The inspirational Mark Hughes led United's attack against Millwall with skill and power, crowning his performance six minutes from time with the winning goal.*

with a clear view of the action, signalled a goal. Robins had done it again!

But Newcastle were far from finished. Five minutes into the second half Mark McGhee was brought down by Steve Bruce. Newcastle were back in the game when he blasted the resulting penalty past Leighton.

Ten minutes later United were in front again. Danny Wallace hit a remarkable goal from the narrowest of angles, smashing the ball into the roof of the net. Now the passion was high and the noise in the stadium deafening.

Newcastle fought back and levelled again when defender Kevin Scott scored, but controversy surrounded the goal. Newcastle took a corner, and as the ball came over Jim Leighton tumbled to the ground. Television clearly showed that the goalkeeper had been tripped by Mick Quinn, but referee Danny Vickers missed the incident and the goal stood.

Would this destroy United? Would that newly-found confidence evaporate? No, back they came again. They had looked a different team all afternoon, and in the 78th minute Brian McClair ended a

personal goal famine with his first success in 17 games. His close-range strike made it 3–2 and the Reds were through.

The Cup win had also given United's form a new complexion: now they had played four matches without defeat – three of them away wins – and all the talk about losing streaks was forgotten.

> 'Because I hadn't scored for a while, getting the winner against Newcastle was obviously a good feeling, especially after the second goal they scored when we felt Jim was impeded. Scoring in front of that noisy crowd made it all the more sweet; every striker likes to get goals under those circumstances. I never give myself a target for scoring a certain number of goals, but obviously I was aware that I wasn't getting them. Perhaps this will change things.
>
> *Brian McClair*

Mark Robins heads the ball into the net for the first of the Reds' three goals against Newcastle.

Brian McClair was delighted to rediscover the goal-scoring habit at St James's Park.

goal after 16 minutes of a game that was almost ruined by gale force winds.

For most of the first half United seemed unable to match anything Chelsea produced and only a brilliant diving save from Jim Leighton kept their lead to one goal by half-time. The second period was totally different. This time Chelsea found the conditions difficult and United were transformed, dominating the play.

Chance after chance came, but the Reds were either off target with their finishing or thwarted by big Dave Beasant in the Chelsea goal. At one point the former Wimbledon and Newcastle 'keeper just managed to get his fingertips to a chip from Brian McClair, turning the ball over the bar. With a smaller goalkeeper it would have been 1–1!

In the end United's frustration was summed up by Mark Hughes, who tried to blast in a goal in the 90th minute instead of tapping the ball in. His shot went wide and United went home without a point.

They were still in 15th place, only two points above third-from-bottom Luton Town, their next opponents. It was crucial that they started to win League games or the Cup run would be meaningless. The Reds had not won a League game at Old Trafford since 12 November – they held their fate in their own hands.

## Saturday 24 February

Defeat did come in the final game of the month, but United were desperately unlucky not to salvage a point at Chelsea. They went behind to a Gareth Hall

### FEBRUARY RESULTS

| | |
|---|---|
| *Manchester United 1* | *Manchester City 1* |
| Blackmore | Brightwell |

| | |
|---|---|
| *Millwall 1* | *Manchester United 2* |
| Morgan | Wallace |
| | Hughes |

| | |
|---|---|
| *Chelsea 1* | *Manchester United 0* |
| Hall | |

### FA CUP
### ROUND 5

| | |
|---|---|
| *Newcastle 2* | *Manchester United 3* |
| McGhee (pen) | Robins |
| Scott | Wallace |
| | McClair |

### LEAGUE POSITION

| P | W | D | L | F | A | Pts | Pos |
|---|---|---|---|---|---|---|---|
| 26 | 7 | 7 | 12 | 30 | 36 | 28 | 15th |

# RED DEVILS' DIARY: March

## Webb back on the glory road

As the grey days of winter came to an end there were hopes among United supporters that the football season still held some promise. True, their favourites struggled in the League and were too close to the relegation zone to sleep easily, but they shared the manager's confidence that the return of the injured players would push them not only to safety, but perhaps to Wembley and success in the FA Cup.

Bryan Robson and Neil Webb were progressing well and expected to play again before the end of the month, and if things went according to plan that would be in time for the semi-final stages of the Cup. Nevertheless, the injury hoodoo that had haunted the club throughout the season persisted as the first game of March drew near. Lee Sharpe went into hospital for a hernia operation and was ruled out of Alex Ferguson's plans for the rest of the season.

*Danny Wallace fires home his contribution to the 4–1 thrashing of Luton.*

It was United's first home win since 12 November, and it certainly left a sweet taste on the lips of the home supporters. United stayed 16th in the table, but the gap above the relegation trio was widening.

### Saturday 3 March

Fellow strugglers Luton Town came to Old Trafford with a certain amount of optimism. They had seen some of the Reds' previous home results, and although they were deep in the relegation zone themselves they perhaps felt that it was their turn to taste victory and avenge their defeat at Kenilworth Road four months earlier.

History was against them, though – no Luton side had beaten United in Manchester since 1897, and that was before Old Trafford was built!

The modern-day Red Devils proved just as formidable as their predecessors in those 93 years and Brian McClair, Mark Hughes, Danny Wallace and Mark Robins ended Luton's dreams in a 4–1 rout.

## Sunday 11 March

Back to the FA Cup for a game many experts predicted would be the end of the Old Trafford dream. The Red Army crossed the Pennines to face high-flying Sheffield United at Bramall Lane. The Second Division side was hotly fancied because of their League success and their style of play.

Managed by Dave 'Harry' Bassett, they had taken the Wimbledon road to glory: under Bassett's guidance Wimbledon had risen through the League to reach the First Division, using the high ball into the penalty area to great effect. The Blades played to the same blueprint. So many critics gathered, expecting to see a giant-killing act. How wrong could they be!

*Mark Hughes in acrobatic form against Luton.*

Sheffield offered very little in the way of resistance, and although there was only one goal, the Reds dominated the game for long periods and the home side rarely threatened. The ranks of United's support had been cut to just 6,000 for safety reasons, but those who made the trip celebrated all the way back to Manchester in a red and white motorcade, no doubt reliving the 29th minute of the game, in which Brian McClair secured their passage into the semi-finals.

The lone goal was due to the persistence of Mark Robins, who chased a loose ball down to the goal-line and managed to hold it in play as Sheffield defenders appealed for a goal kick. Robins won a corner and was on hand as the ball dropped for McClair to head for goal. Sheffield 'keeper Simon Tracey tried to turn the ball over but only managed to deflect it on to the crossbar. As it dropped, McClair recovered his balance and prodded home. Simple but effective!

*Viv Anderson in action against the Blades in the FA Cup sixth round match at Bramall Lane.*

## Wednesday 14 March

With Wembley only a game away United had to concentrate on their League position, and many people were making comparisons with the 1963 season when, under Matt Busby, the team had struggled in the League yet won the FA Cup.

It was a similar story in 1990: new players with a high standard of individual skills were finding it difficult to blend them to put together a run of League wins. But in the Cup it was a different story.

Everton now stood between United and three valuable League points, and the return of Norman Whiteside in the blue of Merseyside was greeted with mixed feelings among the ranks on the terraces. The game itself ended 0–0. Everton played a blanket defence and seemed satisfied to take a point home.

## Sunday 18 March

There were high hopes that United would provide another television spectacular when Liverpool completed the Merseyside double by coming to Old Trafford. There was a buzz of expectancy around the stadium during the first ten minutes of the game, during which United played some good attacking football, but then Liverpool began to dominate and a mistake in the Reds' defence let John Barnes in. The England man ran half the length of the field and slipped the ball past the advancing Jim Leighton.

The United fans were stunned and by the end of the game, when Barnes had added another from the penalty spot and United's only consolation had been an own goal from Ronnie Whelan, they were glad to go home. It had been a miserable performance by United, the complete opposite to their display in the game at Anfield on 23 December. That match had been the last Bryan Robson had played before being side-lined, and those who wondered when he and Neil Webb would return were given the answer on the weekend of the Liverpool debacle. Webb played in the Reserves on 17 March, a well-guarded secret in the United camp, and Robson was ten days behind him in the fitness chase.

## Wednesday 21 March

The first day of spring, but there was no sign of it as United travelled to Hillsborough, home of Ron Atkinson's Sheffield Wednesday.

Webb had played another Reserve game the previous night and it was obvious that his presence would soon be welcomed by his first-team colleagues. There was hope, too, for another player who had been out with a long-term injury: Colin Gibson returned at Sheffield to end a nightmare of injury and illness that had almost ended his career. Not only did he make a comeback, he was also Man of the Match.

But United were awful: they lost 1–0 and could easily have been routed but for the skills of Jim Leighton. The result did nothing for morale. Six points dropped in two games meant that relegation once again loomed. Something had to be done, and quickly.

## Friday 23 March

The United manager normally holds a pre-match conference with the media but after two disappointing defeats Alex decided that there was nothing new he could say, and the interview sessions were cancelled as United left for Southampton.

The fixture list had been cruel – after Liverpool and Wednesday the Reds had to face the First Division's top-scoring team away from home! Neil Webb was back in the squad, and speculation was high that he would play some part in the game.

The next day saw a new United.

## Saturday 24 March

After a quiet start the Reds began to gain ascendancy, and there was a glimmer of hope that they could salvage something. They did – three gold-plated points!

First Colin Gibson consolidated his comeback with a 25-yard shot which bounced just in front of the Saints' 'keeper and into the net. It was Gibson's first goal since April 1988, but during that 23-month period he had started only seven games. Three operations on his knee and an infection which left part of his face paralysed had kept him out of football, but he had refused to be beaten even when some experts advised him to quit the game. He left the field exhausted immediately after scoring and made way for Webb's return. Straight away Neil began to influence the game and it was from his long-range shot that United got their second.

Mark Robins had replaced Mark Hughes, who had played despite a calf strain, and he had been on the field just 30 seconds when he struck. One touch from Robins to Webb and a shot from the midfielder was followed by a cool prod home by the youngster, who took his goal tally to five since his introduction to the side on 30 December.

United won 2–0.

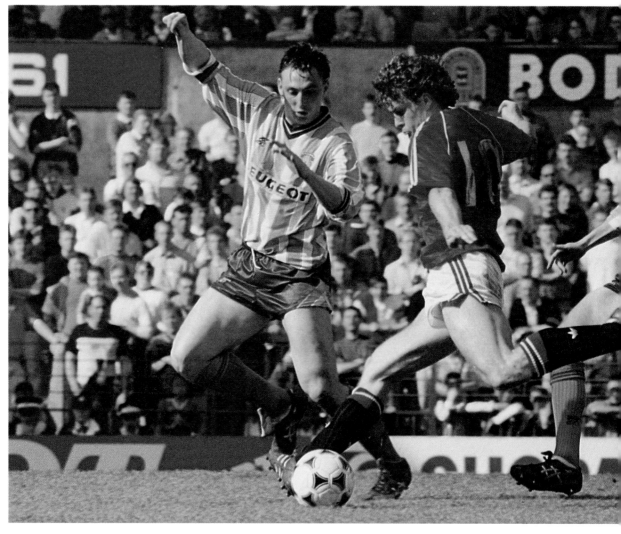

*Neil Webb, who returned to the first team after seven months on the side-lines for the 3–0 defeat of Coventry.*

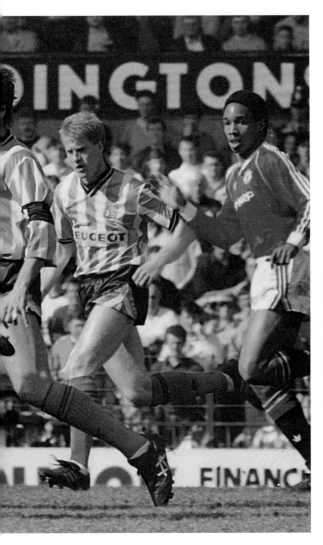

As the fans urged United on the Reds struck in the 26th minute after Paul Ince set up Brian McClair, whose cross was fired home by Mark Hughes.

Nine minutes later 'Sparky' got his second, his 13th League goal of the season, with a powerful right-foot shot from a Webb pass.

Fergie decided on a substitution and Mark Robins replaced Danny Wallace, but it took him 12 minutes to score this time, heading home a Webb corner to put a final touch to the scoring.

Six points in a week had boosted United's League hopes and put them in a good mood for the approaching big game – the FA Cup semi-final against Oldham Athletic. It was just eight days away and everyone knew it was going to be tough.

*Mark Hughes prepares to slam the ball home against Coventry at Old Trafford.*

## Saturday 31 March

The build-up to the next home game was surrounded by speculation that Bryan Robson might make a surprise return. He had played a Reserve match at Coventry four days earlier and had come through the 90 minutes unscathed, but Fergie decided not to risk him against the Coventry senior side.

Instead, as Robson played a morning match in the A team, Neil Webb started his first senior game since 30 August. Although he had been out of action for seven months with an Achilles rupture he was quick to show that his appetite for the game had not subsided.

---

### MARCH RESULTS

| | |
|---|---|
| *Manchester United 4* | *Luton Town 1* |
| McClair | Black |
| Hughes | |
| Wallace | |
| Robins | |

| | |
|---|---|
| *Manchester United 0* | *Everton 0* |

| | |
|---|---|
| *Manchester United 1* | *Liverpool 2* |
| Whelan (og) | Barnes 2 (1 pen) |

| | |
|---|---|
| *Sheffield Wednesday 1* | *Manchester United 0* |
| Hirst | |

| | |
|---|---|
| *Southampton 0* | *Manchester United 2* |
| | Gibson |
| | Robins |

| | |
|---|---|
| *Manchester United 3* | *Coventry City 0* |
| Hughes 2 | |
| Robins | |

### FA CUP

#### ROUND 6

| | |
|---|---|
| *Sheffield United 0* | *Manchester United 1* |
| | McClair |

### LEAGUE POSITION

| P | W | D | L | F | A | Pts | Pos |
|---|---|---|---|---|---|-----|-----|
| 32 | 10 | 8 | 14 | 40 | 40 | 38 | 16th |

# TOP MARKS FOR STUDENT ROBINS

If it were possible to graduate in football skills Mark Robins would have gained an honours degree. To many Mark seemed to be United's find of 1990, but those in the know at Old Trafford had been waiting for the goal-getter to come to the surface after following his progress through the ranks.

Mark was destined for the top right from day one: he is the first pupil from the Football Association's School of Excellence at Lilleshall to make the grade at Old Trafford. It was a tough education and star student Mark had to work hard for his success. 'I always wanted to be a footballer,' he says, 'and my Dad was a United fanatic, so really from as long ago as I can remember there has only been one target, to play for the Reds.'

But hush, don't tell a soul – there's a dark secret in the Robins household. Mark was once upon a time registered as a Junior Blue, a young supporter of – wait for it – Manchester City! 'I never really supported City, but they had the best football team for boys of my age at the time and my father put my name forward', he confesses.

We'll forgive him, but whether City would like to have persuaded Mark to join their ranks remains a well-guarded secret at Maine Road. However, there can be no doubt that he would fit into any side.

'My ambitions to be a footballer led me eventually to Lilleshall, which was just like an ordinary school really, although there was a great deal of concentration on soccer and the various aspects of the game. We lived there, boarding school-style, and did ordinary lessons, but when it came to football that was special. Dave Sexton [the former United manager and England Under-21 coach] was in charge and he was a tremendous help to me.'

After completing his education Mark signed as a young professional with United and immediately began to show his skills. Goals are part of the Robins game and he holds United's record for the most strikes in a season, having netted more than 50 when he was with the Juniors before repeating the feat at Reserve team level a couple of seasons later. If that pattern continues it will mean 50 First Division goals coming up very soon!

Goals follow him around. 'I played my first part of a game at senior level in the Littlewoods Cup tie against

*Mark may once have been a Junior Blue, but there can be no doubting his loyalties now!*

*Goal-scoring hero Robins celebrates his match-winner against Oldham in the FA Cup semi-final replay.*

Rotherham in 1988, and we won 5–0. Actually we were winning 4–0 when I got on the field, and Brian McClair scored the fifth three minutes later!'

There was a long wait for his full debut, which finally came through an emergency switch-around for the FA Cup tie against QPR in January 1989, a month after Mark's 19th birthday. Alex Ferguson made changes as Paul McGrath and Lee Sharpe were forced to pull out at the last minute, and Mark took an unexpected plunge.

His League debut came in the home defeat against Derby County that April, but the game Mark would rather remember was in December 1989, the following season, when he played against Wimbledon at Plough Lane and scored. 'That meant an awful lot to me. I had scored a goal for Manchester United – it was something nobody could ever take away from me.'

Since then the goals have continued to flow for 'on the Mark' Robins, and at one stage in April 1990 he had scored six in six games, five of which he had started as substitute. 'What I never wanted was for everyone to know me as "Super Sub". I'd like to think I have more to offer than that', he says. 'I have worked hard on my game, and not only on finishing but on playing a bigger part in the build-up, and I'm not a

lightweight any more, either. I've gone from ten stone to 12 and grown an inch taller in the last 12 months.'

So what is the secret of the new, improved version of Mark Robins? 'Bobby Charlton told me that when he was a young player he drank a bottle of Guinness every day as he tried to build up his body. I did the same and it worked.'

Well, if that's the recipe for goals galore from Mark Robins in the seasons to come, we'll all drink to that!

*In May Mark scored five goals in his second game for England Under-21s, a 7–3 win over France.*

> 'Mark is like a magnet in the penalty area. He draws the ball towards him and he knows where the target is.'
>
> ## Mark Hughes

*Mark Hughes: praise for his namesake, 'Mark Two'.*

> 'Young Mark is a natural and I'm delighted that he has made it into the first team and overtaken me in the scoring race. That doesn't matter – what does is that he's scoring for us. He has a great deal of natural ability and the striker's secret – being there at the right time. That's so important.'
>
> ## Brian McClair

# RED DEVILS' DIARY: April

## Mark paves the way to Wembley and safety

The first four games of April turned out to be the most significant of the whole season as far as United were concerned – within the space of 17 days their future fate was decided and the Reds had reached Wembley. The team that was, according to some critics, destined for the drop not only secured their First Division status for the next season, but also played a hand in the destiny of the Championship after winning a place in the FA Cup final.

Having reached the semi-finals of the Cup, United found themselves up against their toughest obstacle of the whole season – not even Liverpool at Anfield had proved to be as formidable as Second Division Oldham Athletic at Maine Road. The Latics had long been one of the poor relations among the Manchester clubs, but their achievements during the 1989–90 season ended those hard-up days. The side from the windswept reaches of the outskirts of Greater Manchester was no longer living in the shadow of the big two from the city.

Manchester has always been a place for a night out for Oldham folk. A ten-minute drive takes them past the birthplace of United at Newton Heath before they enter the heart of the city. It was also, for a large majority, the place to watch football, but suddenly in 1990 Boundary Park became the main attraction. Oldham had a team of its own, one which could challenge the best. Former England striker Joe Royle had built a formidable outfit, using the club's plastic pitch to best effect. They feared no one, and when United and Oldham were drawn to face each other in the semi-final of the Cup, there were those who felt that perhaps the buoyant Second Division side would have the advantage over the struggling giants from Old Trafford.

### Sunday 8 April

The Football Association and the BBC tried an experiment. They staged a double bill of semi-finals, Liverpool facing Crystal Palace at Villa Park in a 12.30 kick-off followed by the Oldham–United tie at 3.30 pm.

Football instead of Sunday lunch? The millions who follow the game on television had a feast fit for a thousand kings. First a seven-goal, extra-time thriller saw Steve Coppell's Crystal Palace outwit Liverpool to gain a place at Wembley in a 4–3 victory. Then came United's game.

Viewers hardly had time to catch their breath after the thriller at the Villa when the action switched to Maine Road. There Oldham showed no respect for their rich neighbours, grabbing United by the throat and threatening to kill off any hopes of salvation at the end of a terrible season.

The first goal of the game came from Earl Barrett, a gift from United on Joe Royle's birthday.

Bryan Robson equalised.

United took the lead through Neil Webb.

Oldham made it 2–2 via Ian Marshall.

Play went into extra time, and Danny Wallace gave United the lead, only for Oldham to score two minutes into the second half of the added period through Roger Palmer. It finished 3–3.

## Wednesday 11 April

It was back to Maine Road again for a night to remember. Once again the game was played at a breathtaking pace and for another two hours neither side gave any quarter. Then, just when it looked as if United were going through thanks to a Brian McClair goal, Andy Ritchie equalised and once more extra time had to be played. The additional half-hour produced a moment every United fan will remember for years to come.

Mark Robins, a home-spun player who had been brought on as a substitute, showed ice-cool nerves as he scored the winner. The twist to the tale was that Mark was an Oldham boy. His goal ended his home town's dreams of a double Wembley visit, and the defeat perhaps dashed Oldham's hopes of promotion. They had reached the final of the Littlewoods Cup, in which they lost to Nottingham Forest, then

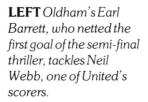

*LEFT* Oldham's Earl Barrett, who netted the first goal of the semi-final thriller, tackles Neil Webb, one of United's scorers.

*Contrasting emotions: coach Jim McGregor hugs match-winner Mark Robins after the replay . . .*

just failed to reach a play-off place.

So United were back at Wembley. But now they had to secure First Division safety. After the Cup win Alex Ferguson found himself in a difficult position. Young Robins had scored five goals in four games and in all of them had come into the action from the substitutes' bench. Fergie was first to admit that Mark had more than earned the opportunity to start a game.

*. . . while goalkeeper Jim Leighton offers quiet consolation to his opposite number, Jon Hallworth.*

## Saturday 14 April

With Mark Robins' name written on the team sheet ahead of his colleagues, United travelled to Queens Park Rangers. Things looked grim: despite that Cup highlight, a real threat of relegation remained,

QPR's goal-scorer, Justin Channing, challenges Steve Bruce.

although the six points they had gained from wins at Southampton and at home to Coventry had helped. The target was 44 points – the Reds had 38, and two more wins would provide safety. There were six games left, three at Old Trafford.

> 'I can't be bothered about Luton Town at the moment. Manchester United have been good enough to take over my contract and I can't have two loyalties. My loyalty has to be to United. They have been good enough to offer me another chance after I've been out of the game for several months, and the fact that our win today, and Luton's defeat, might mean that they go down doesn't really concern me. I'm a Manchester United player, till the end of the season, at least.'
>
> ## Les Sealey
> 14 April

There was a new face in the United line-up: goal-keeper Les Sealey. The tall, dark-haired Londoner found himself in the front line because of an injury to Jim Leighton. With Gary Walsh still injured, and 18-year-old Mark Bosnich the only cover, United had taken Les on loan from Luton.

He had a splendid debut. Beaten by a Justin Channing shot in the 33rd minute, he held out against everything else Rangers could muster and watched his temporary team-mates score twice at the other end. First Mark Robins was on target yet again, and then Neil Webb tapped in from a low Robins cross.

United now had 41 points and, with Charlton and Millwall already relegated, another win would mean total safety.

## Tuesday 17 April

Aston Villa came to Old Trafford with high hopes. They were engaged in a Championship chase with Liverpool and needed to beat United to keep up the pressure. Again Mark Robins started a game and again he showed what a goal-scoring gift he has. He had scored his first senior goal on 30 December. Four months and only ten starts later he reached double figures.

United played perhaps their best football of the season as they outran Villa. Les Sealey had another good game in goal, making a double save from the assaults of former United youngster David Platt, while at the other end Robins sent the home fans wild. He scored both goals in the 2–0 win. In three games he had given United a passage to Wembley and League security. His first strike was a brave diving header from a right wing Wallace cross, and his second goal was one of the highlights of the season.

It was almost half-time as Mark Hughes raced down the right wing, fending off challenges from Villa's desperate defence. Play poured towards the Stretford End. Hughes crossed, and running in from the right hand edge of the penalty area was Robins. The ball bounced to his right, and Robins jumped towards it, letting it pass across his body before he stroked it with the outside of his left foot. It curled high above the outstretched hands of Nigel Spink in the Villa goal and dropped into the net.

Old Trafford erupted. It was a wonder goal, and one well worthy of its importance. It meant that Villa would not win the Championship, and United would not be relegated.

After the two wins, and with First Division football for 1990–91 secured, Alex Ferguson said that although the Cup final was almost a month away the name of Mark Robins was already pencilled in for a place in the Wembley squad. Whether he would start the final was a matter for some consideration!

## Saturday 21 April

The excitement of the previous fortnight had taken its toll when United went to London to face Tottenham Hotspur, where first-half goals from Gascoigne and Lineker brought defeat. The Reds did stage a fight-back, and scored one goal in circumstances which had become unusual for United. They were awarded a penalty, and Steve Bruce scored from the spot kick.

In two seasons the Reds had been awarded just four penalties, a quite remarkable statistic, and of the four they missed two! During 1988–89 season they had one in October and a second in January, then had to wait for the first game of the 1989–90 season for their next. So Brucey hit his third goal of the season, but it was to no avail and the Reds lost their 15th game.

> 'I played club soccer in Australia and was lucky enough to get a trial for Liverpool. I was going to sign for them when United came in. They flew me over to England for a trial and I was so happy with the way I was treated, and the people were so good to me, that I decided to stay here. Alex Ferguson has been like a father to me, he's been great and I've no regrets.'
>
> *Mark Bosnich*
> 30 April

## Monday 30 April

After a nine-day gap United faced three games in six days as the League programme came to an end. Alex Ferguson decided to shuffle the pack. He rested four of his squad and gave another player his debut.

Mark Bosnich faced the big guns of Wimbledon, quite an ordeal for an 18-year-old goalkeeper. The young Aussie gave a solid performance, making three good saves and conquering first-half nerves to keep a clean sheet in a 0–0 draw. The game itself left a lot to be desired, but all thoughts now were of Wembley.

> 'I have to pinch myself to make sure that I'm not dreaming when I think of Wembley and the FA Cup final. It's hard to believe that we've got there at the moment – it still hasn't sunk in as far as I'm concerned. I suppose as we get into Cup final week and the League season is over I'll start to realise that it's true. Wembley, in my first full season as a first-team player – I just can't wait to walk out there . . . if I'm selected!'
>
> *Lee Martin*
> 24 April

> 'Having three games in six days you're asking a lot from players at the end of a season if you want them to battle, and to perform well at Wembley. I'm not going to fall into the trap of over-taxing my side. You only need to look at how tired Oldham were when they lost in the Littlewoods Cup final to see what I mean. It was a tragedy for them after the season they've had. So I'm determined that won't happen to us. I'll use our pool of first-team players the best way I can this week and hopefully they'll all be ready for the final.'
>
> *Alex Ferguson*
> 30 April

### APRIL RESULTS

| | |
|---|---|
| Queens Park Rangers 1 | Manchester United 2 |
| Channing | Robins |
| | Webb |
| | |
| Manchester United 2 | Aston Villa 0 |
| Robins (2) | |
| | |
| Tottenham Hotspur 2 | Manchester United 1 |
| Gascoigne | Bruce (pen) |
| Lineker | |
| | |
| Manchester United 0 | Wimbledon 0 |

#### FA CUP
#### SEMI-FINAL

| | |
|---|---|
| Oldham Athletic 3 | Manchester United 3 (aet) |
| Barrett | Robson |
| Marshall | Webb |
| Palmer | Wallace |

#### SEMI-FINAL (REPLAY)

| | |
|---|---|
| Manchester United 2 | Oldham Athletic 1 (aet) |
| McClair | Ritchie |
| Robins | |

### LEAGUE POSITION

| P | W | D | L | F | A | Pts | Pos |
|---|---|---|---|---|---|-----|-----|
| 36 | 12 | 9 | 15 | 45 | 43 | 45 | 15th |

# SEMI-FINAL DREAM FOR 'GOLDEN BOY' MARK

There has never been a semi-final quite like it: four hours of fantastic football, nine goals and thrills galore as United and Second Division Oldham Athletic battled it out for a place at Wembley in 1990.

The FA Cup has a tradition of conjuring up great moments in football history, but it would be hard to find anything to compare with the clash of two of the North's neighbouring clubs, which twice filled Maine Road in the spring of the new decade. Old Trafford and Oldham's ground at Boundary Park are just a few miles apart across what is nowadays known as Greater Manchester. At one time it would have been an 'all Lancashire' Cup tie, before boundary changes moved the county border to the north of clubs like Bolton, Bury and Rochdale.

So when the draw for the semi-final paired Oldham and United it was regarded very much as a 'local' derby. It was also seen as a difficult game for United.

The Latics were going well. They had reached the final of the Littlewoods Cup to earn their first trip to Wembley, and under the guidance of former England striker Joe Royle they had hopes of making it a double visit – not bad for a club that had never played there before!

In the wake of their Cup trail in both competitions lay their victims: Southampton, Everton, Arsenal, Aston Villa – hardly pushovers . . . would United be next?

There were people who hoped they would, but Fergie's Fighters had other ideas. 'We all know it's going to be a hard game,' said Bryan Robson, 'but if it's going to be hard for us then we intend to make it just as hard for Oldham.' Bryan Robson? Yes, the skipper was back in action just in time to lead his colleagues against Oldham, and the Reds included a fit-again Neil Webb in their squad, too.

As the game approached speculation mounted. Would Fergie risk both the England men who were returning from injury? Would he start with Webb on the field and Robbo as a substitute? Neil had played a

*Robson races away to score United's first goal of the semi-final.*

game and a half before the semi-final while Bryan's build-up had consisted of two Reserve matches and an A team fixture. On the day the United boss opted for experience and picked them both.

Rapturous cheers greeted the Reds as Captain Fantastic led them out for the first time since 23 December 1989. Robbo was back, and within half an hour he showed everyone that nothing had changed.

United lined up: Leighton, Martin, Ince, Pallister, Robson, McClair, Bruce, Webb, Hughes, Gibson, Phelan. On the bench sat Danny Wallace and Mark Robins, neither of whom realised that they would have a crucial role to play in the outcome of the game.

It started badly for United. A couple of forays upfield came to nothing and Oldham showed that their method of defending was to go for the jugular!

United gave away a corner in the fifth minute: the cross came over, there was a scramble and Earl Barrett, a defender who began his career with Manchester City, brought back memories of his days at Maine Road when he prodded the ball home. 1–0 to Oldham. Were they going to do it again? Would another big name go under? Bryan Robson had other ideas.

United slowly began to get back into the game, and in the 29th minute Robson and Webb linked up. The ball broke to Webb, who was playing in a free role in midfield. He glanced up, saw Bryan making a run and timed his pass to perfection. Robson ran forward, beating the offside bid, and shot home. It was 1–1!

The score stayed level beyond half-time, and then it was Webby's turn to stamp his mark on the game. In the 71st minute Robson left the field, making way for Danny Wallace, and it was from the little winger's cross that Neil headed home his first FA Cup goal for United to make it 2–1. Surely Oldham would lie down now!

But no, back they came, and four minutes after United had taken the lead their celebrations were cut short when Ian Marshall, a defender turned striker, rifled home a shot from the left hand edge of the penalty area.

For the first time both the semi-finals had been played 'back to back', and Crystal Palace had beaten Liverpool 4–3 in a game that started three hours before the United–Oldham match. The Reds' supporters had been singing 'Stevie Coppell on the wing', a song from the 1970s, as they began to dream of a final against the club managed by their old favourite. But now they had nothing to sing about as Oldham took the game to United.

The game went into extra time, and Danny Wallace became the hero as he raced through the centre, beating two defenders en route, to slot the ball past 'keeper Jon Hallworth for a 3–2 lead. Surely now that was the end of Latics? Incredibly, the plucky Second Division side fought back once more, and in the 107th minute the score was level again. The scorer this time was Roger Palmer, another former City player enjoying his return to Maine Road.

So after two hours of competitive action referee Joe Worrall brought to an end part one of an epic battle.

Three days later 35,005 turned up for the replay, fewer than Sunday's 44,026 probably because of the nerves of the missing 9,000 would not stand up to the strain! United fielded a changed side – Colin Gibson was dropped to substitute, Michael Phelan switched to right back and Martin to the left. United began the game: Leighton, Phelan, Ince, Pallister, Robson, McClair, Bruce, Webb, Hughes, Martin, Wallace.

Gibson was on the bench alongside Mark Robins, who had taken the field at the end of normal time in the first game and had almost scored. Had he done so he would have realised a dream: 'I was brought up in Oldham, and all my life I have lived in the town', said Mark, whose father is a chief inspector in the Greater Manchester Police. 'We live next door to a Latics supporter who goes everywhere watching them.

'If Oldham win I won't be able to show my face at home for a few days, but nothing would please me more than to get to Wembley with United, and if I can score the goal that takes us there it would be a great experience.'

His chances of doing so looked slim: first he had to get on to the field.

The replay followed a similar pattern to the first encounter, both sides being evenly matched and each creating chances, and at half-time no goals had been scored. Early in the second half Brian McClair forced home a Wallace cross and the United contingent, which far outnumbered the Oldham fans, found the energy to raise their cheers to a new level.

But with ten minutes left it was the turn of the Latics' fans to shout. Andy Ritchie, who began his career with United before being transferred to Brighton, scored an equaliser with a shot from the far post after a free kick was angled across Jim Leighton's goal. After more missed chances for both sides, the whistle blew.

Another 90 minutes played and still no victor, so the game once more went into extra time.

It was then that Alex Ferguson had his last roll of the dice and produced a winning throw. Oldham had used both their substitutes during normal time, and United had pulled off a tiring Neil Webb, who had been replaced by Colin Gibson. Then, ten minutes into the extra period, as Lee Martin was obviously feeling the strain, Fergie sent on Robins.

Within seconds the sturdily-built 20-year-old dashed into the Oldham box, giving clear notice of his intentions. It may have been schoolboy magazine stuff, but Robins was out to score the winner.

United were pressurising Oldham, who had thrown caution to the wind, taking off full-back Andy Barlow to make way for striker Roger Palmer. Earlier they had lost Ian Marshall through injury, his place going to Paul Warhurst, and although the Latics had been forced to alter their plan of action the blueprint remained the same. Attack at all times.

Tension mounted as United poured downfield only to be hit on the rebound by the counter move which forced them to defend. Paul Ince had a magnificent game, and if his performance in the first semi had been his best since his move from West Ham, the display he gave in the replay topped even that.

The stage was set for a dramatic ending and it came in the 111th minute. Mike Phelan, who had also had a good game, collected the ball around the halfway line and began a run down the right side of midfield. He carried the ball forward, fending off the threat from the Oldham defence. The former Norwich man closed in on the Oldham penalty area and pulled back a square pass and there, coming in, was Robins.

Many an experienced player would have panicked under such circumstances but Mark showed his ice-cold temperament, not only controlling the pass but touching the ball forward to tempt Hallworth off his line. The Oldham defence closed in, but with the whole action taking no more than a couple of seconds they had no time to reach Robins and he slotted home the perfect shot.

*A fan shows his appreciation of Mark Robins' winning goal.*

The fans immediately behind the goal were stunned, for that was where the Oldham section sat. The rest of Maine Road erupted. United were through, thanks to Mark Robins! The United players besieged Mark, burying him under a mass of red shirts. When he emerged, chest out, he was smiling broadly and punching the night air in celebration. It was a killer blow, but Oldham just would not lie down.

Right to the last they fought, and just as referee Worrall was about to end the marathon, they came

*The United bench celebrate victory in what Fergie described as 'one of the best semi-finals of all time'.*

within a hair's breadth of forcing a third game. Andy Ritchie looked yards offside as he broke away to pick up a ball on the left, and his chip was going into the top corner of Jim Leighton's goal when somehow the 'keeper found an extra centimetre of reach, turning the effort over the angle of bar and post.

The final whistle went and some United supporters found the occasion too much. They spilled on to the field, ignoring warnings to stay clear, and hoisted Mark Robins shoulder high. There were some remarkable scenes as Steve Bruce had his shirt torn off by a souvenir hunter, and players and fans hugged one another in ecstasy.

The Oldham players left the field in despair, some weeping from the frustration of defeat. Oldham's heroes left the dressing-room quickly and quietly to run the media gauntlet, while United stayed on behind closed doors, no doubt reliving the highs of the previous two hours.

For Alex Ferguson it was a moment to cherish: 'That must be one of the best semi-finals of all time. It's a great moment for me to get through to my first English Cup final, but I have only praise for the way both sets of players approached these games. They were magnificent. As far as I am concerned Oldham are the best team we have played this season and the attitude and sportsmanship shown was so good for the game. There was no nastiness, no gamesmanship, nothing other than good, honest football and Joe Royle must be as proud of his players as I am of mine'.

As for Mark Robins, he could be forgiven for having to pinch himself to make sure that he had not been dreaming. 'I'm delighted that we are through to Wembley. Now it's my ambition to take some part in the Cup final, and if I could score a goal in that game it really would be the end of the greatest year in my life so far. How do I feel right now? I know it's a cliché, but I can't think of any other way to describe it. I'm over the moon!' An old footballing expression from one of the game's newest stars, and United were bound for Wembley.

# START THE DAY THE PHELAN WAY

There is nothing Michael Phelan likes better than to start the day with a bacon butty! The United midfielder who has developed into a utility player since his big-money move from Norwich City is a down-to-earth man whose regular breakfast order when the team is away from home sums up his approach to life. 'Two slices of bread with some nicely grilled bacon between them, you can't beat it', he says in his rich Lancashire accent.

Mike is a northerner through and through, raised in Nelson in true Lancashire country. He watched his football at Burnley's Turf Moor ground as a youngster, dreaming of the day when he might wear the claret and blue of the one-time First Division giants.

'When I was a lad there was only one team for me, and my thoughts were all on making it to the top with Burnley. I know that Old Trafford wasn't so very far away but it might just as well have been on another planet as far as the folk in Burnley were concerned. We have our own town, our own way of life and our own football team, and there's a passion for the game up there. It's a pity that they can't get back to the top because there is so much support bubbling away under the surface in Burnley, just waiting for the chance to follow a successful side.'

Mike's route to success has the hint of a mystery tour about it. He covered the 30-odd miles from Burnley to Old Trafford by the long route – via

*Michael Phelan set his sights on a career at the top, but he travelled the long way round from Burnley to Manchester – via Norwich!*

Norwich! After success at school football, young Michael Phelan achieved his ambition and was signed by Burnley, tasting success and failure during his time at the club. 'We were in the Second Division when I joined. A few years later, by the time I was breaking into the first team, we were relegated. Two seasons later we were Third Division champions and then went down again.'

The successful side began to break up and players like Mike, Trevor Steven and Brian Laws became the targets of bigger clubs. So it was bacon butties for breakfast in Norwich that came next for Michael P.! 'It was quite a wrench leaving my home area to go as far away as Norwich,' he says, 'but the aim of every professional footballer has to be to better himself, and as far as I was concerned it was a step up the ladder. I was in the side which won the Second Division in 1986 and a season later we finished fifth in Division 1.'

Eventually he caught the eye of Alex Ferguson, and in the summer of 1989 he joined United in a £750,000 deal. 'That was a great moment. Obviously moving back to the north pleased my family, but joining a club like United gave me a tremendous feeling of personal satisfaction.

'I know I supported Burnley as a kid, but playing for a club like Manchester United is a distant dream for any schoolboy. I always admired players at Old Trafford, and I suppose it was always an ambition to play for a club like this, but you have to be realistic.'

But Michael Phelan made it, signing for United in a double deal – Neil Webb added his name to a contract

on the same day. 'It was an unforgettable moment. There were more media people around that day than we saw in a whole season at Norwich. You would have thought that United had just won the title or something like that. Cameras, microphones, reporters everywhere – it was then that I realised what a big club I had signed for.'

And Old Trafford itself? 'What a stadium! Looking around you can see what a terrific place it is and the atmosphere, even when the ground is empty, sends a tingle right through you.'

There was no prouder man than Michael Phelan as he walked up the Wembley tunnel after the Cup final win. He could look back on his first season at Old Trafford with a certain amount of satisfaction. After his debut on the opening day against Arsenal he played in all but one game throughout the season, missing the Cup tie at Hereford because of injury.

Holding his winners' medal, he said : 'Winning this has more than made up for the disappointments we've suffered during the season. We hoped for so much at the start, and I was sure that we were going to be in with a chance of taking the Championship, but it wasn't to be. We had a fight on our hands, but we all knew we wouldn't go down, just as we knew that we could win the Cup. This is a great moment, and the perfect way to end your first season at a club. I hope there'll be many more moments like it!'

Then he was off to celebrate. A glass of champagne, and perhaps something a little more splendid than a bacon butty . . . but then again perhaps not.

# RED DEVILS' DIARY: May

## Wobbles before Wembley

By the time the last month of the season arrived United were safe from relegation and preparing for the FA Cup final, and the internationals in the squad were flexing their muscles for the World Cup. The Cup final had provided United with a face-saving end to the season, and for two key players there was another target.

Bryan Robson and Neil Webb had both recovered from their injury problems in time to make it for an England get-together at the end of April when Czechoslovakia came to England to provide the opposition for games at both B and full levels. Neil needed as much football as posible to build up his fitness and to try to secure a place in the England party for Italy, and he took advantage of a run-out in the B game, playing for 75 minutes. The following day Bryan led out England for the first time in 1990 and played three-quarters of a game. Eventually both players were named in the World Cup squad.

As for the Scotland players, Jim Leighton sat out the friendly against East Germany, a move which had been agreed beforehand. Jim had been due to stand down a month earlier, but Hibs' 'keeper Andy Goram dislocated a finger in training and so Jim played in the Scots' victory over Argentina. Brian McClair's important Cup goals for United had not secured his place in the Scottish squad and he was later to learn that he was not included in the World Cup party.

But now the rush for Cup final tickets was on. For the first time, United's membership scheme played a role in the distribution. As Wembley's capacity had been cut to an all-seater 80,000 there were fewer tickets given to the finalists than in previous years, and because of this most went to United club members. As always the ticket allocations sparked off a row. The FA decided that the share-out would be based on the average home attendances of the two finalists over the previous three years. United were given 24,000, while Crystal Palace received 17,000.

## Tuesday 2 May

The United players reported to the Cliff for light training as they prepared for the trip to Nottingham the following day. It was the night after a 0–0 home draw against Wimbledon, which had been watched by Old Trafford's smallest League gate of the season – 29,281 – 6,000 up on the same fixture the previous year.

For the Forest game Fergie decided to shuffle his pack. Four regulars had been rested against the Dons, and as the manager wrote his team-sheet for the Nottingham trip he decided to repeat this game plan, leaving out Mark Hughes, Bryan Robson, Paul Ince and Lee Martin. It was a decision which was to have a devastating effect.

> 'Perhaps the fact that we were safe from relegation had some effect on our performances during the last weeks of the season, but my meddling with the team was to blame, too. You like to keep the same side as often as possible, but I had to look at the fact that we were playing three games in six days, and that's asking a lot at this time of the season. That's why I rested players for the games against Wimbledon and Forest.'
>
> **Alex Ferguson**
> 3 May

## Wednesday 3 May

The game against Forest got off to a lively start and in the first minute Brian McClair came close to scoring. His shot curled over Mark Crossley, who seemed to have difficulty seeing it in the bright sunshine, but he got a last-second touch and turned the ball over for a corner.

Next Danny Wallace was presented with a clear shot at goal and blasted the ball high into the terraces . . . then things started to go wrong. Forest had four shots at goal in the next 23 minutes and United found themselves 4–0 down!

> 'It was an unbelievable game to play in. We seemed to start off OK, but then they had a shot from 25 yards and it screamed in. After that they got three goals which left us wondering what had hit us. We made elementary mistakes and found ourselves 4–0 down after 25 minutes. We felt totally embarrassed and Forest just couldn't believe their luck.'
>
> **Steve Bruce**
> *After the Nottingham Forest match*

The game was a total disaster. Forest fought like tigers, United were humiliated and Fergie was furious. So angry was the United boss that he refused to make a substitution, allowing Viv Anderson and Paul Ince to sit it out on the bench as those who had caused the embarrassment were forced to endure the next 45 minutes. Luckily, there were no more goals for Forest – but none for United, either.

A night to remember for Forest, certainly one to forget for the Reds.

## Saturday 5 May

The curtain came down on the League campaign as a crowd of just under 40,000 welcomed relegated Charlton Athletic to Old Trafford. There was a carnival atmosphere to the game although the football left a lot to be desired.

Speculation was high that the team fielded for this match would be the one to face Crystal Palace in the Cup final seven days later, although Fergie refused to admit this. The Reds lined up: Leighton, Phelan, Pallister, Bruce, Martin, Webb, Robson, Ince, Wallace, McClair, Hughes, with Mal Donaghy and Mark Robins as substitutes.

*Gary Pallister, who scored the winner against Charlton in a carnival atmosphere at Old Trafford.*

Gary Pallister scored the winner, blasting home a shot after goalkeeper Bob Bolder palmed out a Steve Bruce header. The highlight of the game, though, was the behaviour of both sets of supporters. True, Charlton offered little threat to United's status, but the Reds' fans chanted 'You'll be back', as the visitors replied, 'We hope you win the Cup'. They danced the conga and joined in a Mexican wave, showing a face of football which was in sharp contrast to the one that hit the headlines the following day.

## Sunday 6 May

As UEFA were on the point of lifting the ban on English clubs the game was dealt a body-blow by rampaging Leeds supporters. Thousands ran riot in Bournemouth while their team, led by ex-United star Gordon Strachan, won promotion as Second Division Champions. Would the cup-winners now get back into Europe?

## Wednesday 9 May

United were in a relaxed mood as the players gathered at a Cheshire hotel. Alex Ferguson had broken with tradition by staying in Manchester during the build-up to Wembley rather than moving into the London area four or five days before the big game.

## Thursday 10 May

United arrived at their Buckinghamshire base to find that they were not alone: they were sharing the hotel with the full England squad, assembled there for a friendly against Denmark three days after the final!

## Friday 11 May

Following a training session at nearby Bisham Abbey, Alex Ferguson held his last press conference before the final. Television cameras covered his every word, photographers gathered the players together for yet more pictures and then the doors were closed.

Fergie named his Wembley squad and it *was* the 11 who had started against Charlton, plus Mark Robins and Clayton Blackmore. United were ready for Wembley.

> 'It was a lacklustre performance but at least we got three points, and that's the right way to end the season. I was delighted to score, and it's a pity that it was the only goal of the game because the crowd deserved more. Steve Bruce made the goal with a terrific header and the 'keeper managed to pull off a great save. It ricocheted to me and when it fell on my left tab I thought, oh, no not that leg. But I managed to get a shot in and it went home'.
>
> **Gary Pallister**
> *After the Charlton Athletic match*

**TOP** *No, it's not the men from Mars! United line up for a photocall in Cheshire before the big day.*

**BOTTOM** *Red Devils Ince and Webb are ready for Wembley and Crystal Palace.*

## MAY RESULTS

| | |
|---|---|
| Nottingham Forest 4 | Manchester United 0 |
| Parker | |
| Pearce | |
| Clough | |
| Chettle | |

| | |
|---|---|
| Manchester United 1 | Charlton Athletic 0 |
| Pallister | |

## FINAL LEAGUE POSITION

| P | W | D | L | F | A | Pts | Pos |
|---|---|---|---|---|---|-----|-----|
| 38 | 13 | 9 | 16 | 46 | 47 | 48 | 13th |

## FA CUP
### FINAL

| | |
|---|---|
| Crystal Palace 3 | Manchester United 3 (aet) |
| O'Reilly | Robson |
| Wright (2) | Hughes (2) |

### REPLAY

| | |
|---|---|
| Manchester United 1 | Crystal Palace 0 |
| Martin | |

# HEARTBREAK FOR JIM AS LES EARNS GOLD

'Sealey! Sealey', chanted the United section of the Wembley crowd. The masses hailed a new hero as Bryan Robson climbed the 39 steps to collect the FA Cup for a record third time. The air was full of the sound of celebration. United had won the Cup, but Les Sealey's thoughts were elsewhere.

The Luton Town goalkeeper had been called into the United side 24 hours before the replayed 1990 FA Cup final when Alex Ferguson placed his job on the line in an incredible gamble. For four days Fergie wrestled with the biggest problem of his managerial career. Jim Leighton had been his regular goalkeeper for years – Fergie had given the young Scot his break at Aberdeen and persuaded the mature international

*Les Sealey, on loan from Luton, helped United out of the relegation zone in two crucial matches.*

to join United shortly after his 30th birthday. Moving south had been a gamble for Jim, and now the United manager had to take an even bigger risk.

In the original final on 12 May, Jim found himself under the microscope. The big occasion of an English Cup final appeared to affect his performance and the blemishes were exposed by television. Fergie could not risk that happening again in the replay, so for days he tossed over the idea of bringing in his on-loan 'keeper.

Sealey had played just two senior games in the entire 1989–90 season, both crucial to United's future, and he was on the winning side on both occasions. With Les in goal the Reds beat QPR at Loftus Road and Aston Villa at Old Trafford, clawing their way out of the relegation zone as well as ending Villa's championship hopes.

So on Wednesday 16 May, manager Ferguson decided the time had come. There had been plenty of speculation following the 3–3 draw the previous Saturday, stories sparked off by the fact that United had rushed through an extension to Sealey's loan period. This had elapsed after the original final and they needed to re-register him so that he would be eligible for the Thursday evening replay. Cover for Jim Leighton? Perhaps. There were those who speculated that Sealey was destined to play against Crystal Palace in that game and they guessed right.

The players were relaxing in the quiet surroundings of their Buckinghamshire hideaway at Burnham Beeches. They had trained that morning and were about to go for their evening meal when Alex called a team meeting. Before it began he took Jim to one side to tell him that he would be the odd man out for the Cup final replay. Leighton was stunned.

Alex Ferguson knew he was taking a massive gamble. If Les Sealey had a bad game and Crystal Palace won the Cup the manager's job could even be on the line. By dropping Jim Leighton for such a crucial game he might even affect the goalkeeper's

*A dejected Jim Leighton remained on the side-lines for the FA Cup final replay.*

final whistle rewarded his confident performance. He climbed the steps to where the Duke and Duchess of Kent welcomed the winning side and received a winners' medal ... but his thoughts were of Jim Leighton, who was now sitting alone in the dressing-room, trying to shut out the sounds of the celebrations which echoed around him.

Sealey slipped away from the lap of honour, brushed aside microphones and requests for interviews and strode up the sloping walkway which forms Wembley's famous players' tunnel. His face was expressionless as he passed the team coaches parked nose to tail in the bowels of the stadium and turned left, passing through the dressing-room door.

Then, unwitnessed, he made a presentation of his own. Les Sealey handed Jim Leighton his Cup-winners' medal. The two men shook hands to share an unforgettable moment and the despair of Jim Leighton was briefly eased. The stand-in goalkeeper's gesture was recognised by Alex Ferguson as being 'typical of the man'.

Sealey was rewarded with a 12-month contract at Old Trafford, and the FA announced that because Jim Leighton had played in the original final he had already qualified for a medal which would be sent on to him.

So Les got his medal after all.

chances of being picked for the Scotland squad for the World Cup, and would put his future at Old Trafford in doubt. These were risks he knew he had to take. Fergie stood by his decision and Sealey played.

He kept a clean sheet as United won the Cup, and the cries of 'Sealey, Sealey' which went up after the

*Andy Gray's free kick was no match for Les Sealey, who kept a clean sheet in the FA Cup final victory.*

# MANCHESTER UNITED: HOW THEY LINED UP

How they lined up. Here is a complete breakdown of every United game played during the 1989–90 season, showing who played, who scored, and how many watched the game. The chart also gives half-time and full-time scores and United's position in the League after each game.

| | Ven | Att | H/T | Res | | 1 | 2 | 3 | 4 | 5 |
|---|---|---|---|---|---|---|---|---|---|---|
| **August** | | | | | | | | | | |
| 19 Arsenal | H | 47,245 | 1–1 | 4–1 | — | Leighton | Duxbury | Blackmore | **Bruce** | Phelan |
| 22 C Palace | A | 22,423 | 1–0 | 1–1 | — | ,, | ,, | ,, | ,, | ,, |
| 26 Derby Co | A | 22,175 | 0–1 | 0–2 | — | ,, | ,, | Martin | ,, | ,, |
| 30 Norwich C | H | 39,610 | 0–1 | 0–2 | 15 | ,, | ,, | Blackmore | ,, | ,, |
| **September** | | | | | | | | | | |
| 9 Everton | A | 37,916 | 0–1 | 2–3 | 16 | ,, | ,, | Martin | ,, | ,, |
| 16 Millwall | H | 42,476 | 2–1 | 5–1 | 11 | ,, | Anderson | Donaghy | ,, | ,, |
| *Littlewoods Cup* | | | | | | | | | | |
| 20 Portsmouth | A | 18,072 | 3–0 | 3–2 | R2(1) | ,, | ,, | ,, | Beardsmore | ,, |
| 23 Manchester C | A | 43,246 | 0–3 | 1–5 | 14 | ,, | ,, | ,, | Duxbury | ,, |
| **October** | | | | | | | | | | |
| *Littlewoods Cup* | | | | | | | | | | |
| 3 Portsmouth | H | 26,698 | 0–0 | 0–0 | R2(2) | ,, | Duxbury | ,, | Bruce | ,, |
| 14 Sheffield Weds | H | 41,492 | 0–0 | 0–0 | 17 | ,, | ,, | ,, | ,, | ,, |
| 21 Coventry C | A | 19,605 | 2–0 | 4–1 | 14 | ,, | Donaghy | Martin | **Bruce** | **Phelan** |
| *Littlewoods Cup* | | | | | | | | | | |
| 25 Tottenham H | H | 45,759 | 0–1 | 0–3 | R3 | ,, | ,, | ,, | ,, | ,, |
| 28 Southampton | H | 37,122 | 1–1 | 2–1 | 11 | ,, | ,, | ,, | ,, | ,, |
| **November** | | | | | | | | | | |
| 4 Charlton Ath | A | 16,065 | 0–0 | 0–2 | 13 | ,, | ,, | ,, | ,, | ,, |
| 12 Nottingham F | H | 34,184 | 1–0 | 1–0 | 11 | ,, | Blackmore | ,, | ,, | ,, |
| 18 Luton T | A | 11,141 | 2–0 | 3–1 | 9 | ,, | **Blackmore** | ,, | ,, | ,, |
| 25 Chelsea | H | 47,106 | 0–0 | 0–0 | 10 | ,, | ,, | ,, | ,, | ,, |
| **December** | | | | | | | | | | |
| 3 Arsenal | A | 34,484* | 0–1 | 0–1 | 12 | ,, | ,, | ,, | ,, | ,, |
| 9 C Palace | H | 33,514 | 1–1 | 1–2 | 12 | ,, | **Beardsmore** | ,, | ,, | ,, |
| 16 Tottenham H | H | 36,230 | 0–0 | 0–1 | 13 | ,, | ,, | Sharpe | ,, | ,, |
| 23 Liverpool | A | 37,426 | 0–0 | 0–0 | 12 | ,, | Blackmore | Martin | ,, | ,, |
| 26 Aston Villa | A | 41,247 | 0–0 | 0–3 | 16 | ,, | Anderson | ,, | ,, | ,, |
| 30 Wimbledon | A | 9,622 | 0–1 | 2–2 | 15 | ,, | ,, | ,, | ,, | ,, |
| **January** | | | | | | | | | | |
| 1 QPR | H | 34,824 | 0–0 | 0–0 | 15 | ,, | ,, | ,, | ,, | ,, |
| *FA Cup* | | | | | | | | | | |
| 7 Nottingham F | A | 23,072 | 0–0 | 1–0 | R3 | ,, | ,, | ,, | ,, | ,, |
| 13 Derby Co | H | 38,985 | 0–1 | 1–2 | 15 | ,, | ,, | ,, | *sent off* | ,, |
| 21 Norwich C | A | 17,370 | 0–0 | 0–2 | 17 | ,, | ,, | ,, | ,, | ,, |

| 6 | 7 | 8 | 9 | 10 | 11 | 12 | 14 |
|---|---|---|---|---|---|---|---|
| Donaghy | Robson | **Webb** | **McClair** | **Hughes** | Sharpe | Martin (11) | Robins |
| ,, | **Robson** | ,, | ,, | ,, | ,, | Martin | Milne |
| Blackmore | ,, | ,, | ,, | ,, | ,, | Milne | Graham (3) |
| Pallister | ,, | ,, | ,, | ,, | ,, | Martin (7) | Robins (3) |
| ,, | Donaghy | Blackmore | **McClair** | ,, | ,, | Anderson (2) | **Beardsmore** (3) |
| ,, | **Robson** | Ince | ,, | **Hughes (3)** | **Sharpe** | Duxbury (8) | Beardsmore (4) |
| ,, | ,, | **Ince (2)** | ,, | ,, | **Wallace** | Duxbury (7) | Sharpe (9) |
| ,, | Beardsmore | ,, | ,, | **Hughes** | Wallace | Sharpe (7) | Blackmore |
| ,, | Robson | ,, | ,, | ,, | ,, | Blackmore, | Sharpe |
| ,, | ,, | ,, | ,, | ,, | ,, | Martin (2) | Sharpe (11) |
| ,, | ,, | ,, | ,, | **Hughes (2)** | Sharpe | Duxbury (8) | Maiorana (11) |
| ,, | ,, | ,, | ,, | ,, | ,, | Duxbury | Maiorana (3) |
| ,, | ,, | ,, | **McClair (2)** | ,, | ,, | Blackmore (8) | Maiorana |
| ,, | ,, | ,, | ,, | ,, | ,, | Blackmore (11) | Wallace (2) |
| **Pallister** | ,, | ,, | ,, | ,, | Wallace | Beardsmore | Sharpe (11) |
| ,, | ,, | ,, | ,, | **Hughes** | **Wallace** | Beardsmore | Sharpe |
| ,, | ,, | ,, | ,, | ,, | ,, | Duxbury (3) | Beardsmore (11) |
| ,, | ,, | ,, | ,, | ,, | ,, | Beardsmore (2) | Donaghy |
| ,, | ,, | ,, | ,, | Sharpe | ,, | Hughes (10) | Blackmore (5) |
| ,, | ,, | ,, | ,, | Hughes | ,, | Anderson (4) | Blackmore (2) |
| ,, | ,, | ,, | ,, | ,, | ,, | Anderson | Sharpe (11) |
| ,, | Blackmore | ,, | ,, | ,, | Sharpe | Duxbury (3) | Robins (7) |
| ,, | ,, | ,, | ,, | **Hughes** | **Robins** | Duxbury | Sharpe (8) |
| ,, | Sharpe | Blackmore | ,, | ,, | ,, | Duxbury (7) | Beardsmore (8) |
| ,, | Beardsmore | ,, | ,, | ,, | **Robins** | Duxbury (8) | Milne |
| **Pallister** | ,, | ,, | ,, | ,, | ,, | Duxbury (8) | Milne (7) |
| ,, | Robins | Ince | ,, | ,, | Wallace | Blackmore (5) | Beardsmore (8) |

| | Ven | Att | H/T | Res | | 1 | 2 | 3 | 4 | 5 |
|---|---|---|---|---|---|---|---|---|---|---|
| **FA Cup** | | | | | | | | | | |
| 28 Hereford U | A | 13,777 | 0–0 | 1–0 | R4 | Leighton | Anderson | Martin | Donaghy | Duxbury |
| **February** | | | | | | | | | | |
| 3 Manchester C | H | 40,274 | 0–0 | 1–1 | 17 | ,, | ,, | ,, | ,, | Phelan |
| 10 Millwall | A | 15,491 | 0–1 | 2–1 | 15 | ,, | ,, | ,, | Beardsmore | ,, |
| **FA Cup** | | | | | | | | | | |
| 18 Newcastle U | A | 31,748 | 1–0 | 3–2 | R5 | ,, | ,, | ,, | Bruce | ,, |
| 24 Chelsea | A | 29,979 | 0–1 | 0–1 | 16 | ,, | ,, | ,, | ,, | ,, |
| **March** | | | | | | | | | | |
| 3 Luton T | H | 35,237 | 3–0 | 4–1 | 16 | ,, | ,, | ,, | ,, | ,, |
| **FA Cup** | | | | | | | | | | |
| 11 Sheffield U | A | 34,500 | 1–0 | 1–0 | R6 | ,, | ,, | ,, | ,, | ,, |
| 14 Everton | H | 37,398 | 0–0 | 0–0 | 16 | ,, | Duxbury | ,, | ,, | ,, |
| 18 Liverpool | H | 46,629 | 0–1 | *1–2 | 16 | ,, | Anderson | ,, | ,, | ,, |
| 21 Sheffield Weds | A | 33,260 | 0–1 | 0–1 | 16 | ,, | Donaghy | ,, | ,, | ,, |
| 24 Southampton | A | 20,510 | 0–0 | 2–0 | 16 | ,, | ,, | ,, | ,, | ,, |
| 31 Coventry C | H | 39,172 | 2–0 | 3–0 | 16 | ,, | ,, | Gibson | ,, | ,, |
| **April** | | | | | | | | | | |
| *FA Cup semi-final* | | | | | | | | | | |
| 8 Oldham Ath | MR | 44,026 | 1–1 | 2–2 | 3–3* | ,, | Martin | ,, | ,, | ,, |
| *FA Cup s/f Replay* | | | | | | | | | | |
| 11 Oldham Ath | MR | 35,005 | 0–0 | 2–1 | *aet | ,, | Ince | Martin | ,, | ,, |
| 14 QPR | A | 18,997 | 0–1 | 2–1 | 14 | Sealey | ,, | ,, | ,, | ,, |
| 17 Aston Villa | H | 44,080 | 2–0 | 2–0 | 13 | ,, | Anderson | Gibson | **Robins (2)** | ,, |
| 21 Tottenham H | A | 33,317 | 0–2 | 1–2 | 14 | Leighton | Robins | Martin | **Bruce** (*pen*) | ,, |
| 30 Wimbledon | H | 29,281 | 0–0 | 0–0 | 15 | Bosnich | Anderson | ,, | ,, | ,, |
| **May** | | | | | | | | | | |
| 2 Nottingham F | A | 21,186 | 0–4 | 0–4 | 16 | Leighton | Duxbury | Blackmore | ,, | ,, |
| 5 Charlton Ath | H | 35,389 | 1–0 | 1–0 | 13 | ,, | Ince | Martin | ,, | ,, |
| **FA Cup final** | | | | | | | | | | |
| 12 C Palace | W | 80,000 | 1–1 | 2–2 | 3–3* | ,, | ,, | ,, | ,, | ,, |
| **FA Cup final replay** | | | | | | | | | | |
| 17 C Palace | W | 80,000 | 0–0 | 1–0 | | Sealey | ,, | **Martin** | ,, | ,, |

| 6 | 7 | 8 | 9 | 10 | 11 | 12 | 14 |
|---|---|---|---|---|---|---|---|
| Pallister | **Blackmore** | Ince | McClair | Hughes | Wallace | Beardsmore (8) | Robins |
| ,, | **Blackmore** | Duxbury | ,, | ,, | ,, | Beardsmore (4) | Robins (11) |
| ,, | ,, | ,, | ,, | **Hughes** | **Wallace** | Brazil (2) | Robins (7) |
| ,, | **Robins** | ,, | **McClair** | ,, | **Wallace** | Ince (8) | Beardsmore (7) |
| ,, | Duxbury | Ince | ,, | ,, | ,, | Donaghy (2) | Beardsmore (7) |
| ,, | **Robins** | ,, | **McClair** | Hughes | Wallace | Duxbury | Beardsmore (11) |
| ,, | ,, | ,, | **McClair** | ,, | ,, | Duxbury (2) | Beardsmore |
| ,, | ,, | ,, | ,, | ,, | ,, | Blackmore (7) | Beardsmore (10) |
| ,, | Blackmore | ,, | ,, | ,, | ,, | Duxbury (2) | Beardsmore (11) |
| ,, | Beardsmore | Gibson | ,, | ,, | Blackmore | Ince (11) | Wallace (7) |
| ,, | **Gibson** | Ince | ,, | ,, | Wallace | Webb (7) | **Robins** (10) |
| ,, | Webb | ,, | ,, | **Hughes (2)** | ,, | Martin (2) | **Robins** (11) |
| ,, | **Robson** | ,, | ,, | ,, | **Webb** | **Wallace** (7) | Robins (2) |
| ,, | ,, | Webb | **McClair** | ,, | Wallace | Gibson (8) | **Robins** (3) |
| ,, | ,, | **Webb** | ,, | ,, | ,, | Gibson (4) | **Robins** (10) |
| ,, | ,, | ,, | ,, | ,, | ,, | Blackmore (3) | Beardsmore (2) |
| ,, | ,, | ,, | ,, | ,, | ,, | Blackmore (8) | Beardsmore (11) |
| ,, | Beardsmore | Ince | Robins | ,, | Gibson | Wallace (9) | Blackmore (11) |
| ,, | ,, | Webb | McClair | Robins | Wallace | Ince | Anderson |
| **Pallister** | Robson | ,, | ,, | Hughes | ,, | Donaghy | Robins |
| ,, | **Robson** | ,, | ,, | **Hughes (2)** | ,, | Robins (6) | Blackmore (3) |
| ,, | ,, | ,, | ,, | ,, | ,, | Robins | Blackmore |

*Bryan Robson*

*Paul Ince*

# STATISTICIANS UNITE!
## Everything you need to know about season 1989-90

Here it is . . . the complete guide to United's Cup-winning series, and a breakdown of goal-scorers, appearances and attendances. It's the perfect record for any Reds supporter and perhaps the first step along the road to becoming a statistician yourself.

### BARCLAYS FOOTBALL LEAGUE DIVISION I

| Date | Ven | Opponents | H/T | Res | Lg/pos | Scorers | Att |
|------|-----|-----------|-----|-----|--------|---------|-----|
| **August** | | | | | | | |
| 19 | H | Arsenal | 1–1 | 4–1 | — | Bruce, Hughes, Webb, McClair | 47,245 |
| 22 | A | C Palace | 1–0 | 1–1 | — | Robson | 22,423 |
| 26 | A | Derby Co | 0–1 | 0–2 | — | | 22,175 |
| 30 | H | Norwich C | 0–1 | 0–2 | 15 | | 39,610 |
| **September** | | | | | | | |
| 9 | A | Everton | 0–1 | 2–3 | 16 | McClair, Beardsmore | 37,916 |
| 16 | H | Millwall | 2–1 | 5–1 | 12 | Hughes(3), Robson, Sharpe | 42,476 |
| 23 | A | Manchester C | 0–3 | 1–5 | 14 | Hughes | 43,246 |
| **October** | | | | | | | |
| 14 | H | Sheffield Weds | 0–0 | 0–0 | 17 | | 41,492 |
| 21 | A | Coventry C | 2–0 | 4–1 | 14 | Bruce, Hughes(2), Phelan | 19,605 |
| 28 | H | Southampton | 1–1 | 2–1 | 11 | McClair(2) | 37,122 |
| **November** | | | | | | | |
| 4 | A | Charlton Ath | 0–0 | 0–2 | 13 | | 16,065 |
| 12 | H | Nottingham F | 1–0 | 1–0 | 11 | Pallister | 34,184 |
| 18 | A | Luton T | 2–0 | 3–1 | 9 | Wallace, Blackmore, Hughes | 11,141 |
| 25 | H | Chelsea | 0–0 | 0–0 | 10 | | 47,106 |
| **December** | | | | | | | |
| 3 | A | Arsenal | 0–1 | 0–1 | 12 | | 34,484 |
| 9 | H | C Palace | 1–1 | 1–2 | 12 | Beardsmore | 33,514 |
| 16 | H | Tottenham H | 0–0 | 0–1 | 13 | | 36,230 |
| 23 | A | Liverpool | 0–0 | 0–0 | 12 | | 37,426 |
| 26 | A | Aston Villa | 0–0 | 0–3 | 16 | | 41,247 |
| 30 | A | Wimbledon | 0–1 | 2–2 | 15 | Hughes, Robins | 9,622 |

| Date | Ven | Opponents | H/T | Res | Lg/pos | Scorers | Att |
|------|-----|-----------|-----|-----|--------|---------|-----|
| **January** | | | | | | | |
| 1 | H | QPR | 0–0 | 0–0 | 15 | | 34,824 |
| 13 | H | Derby Co | 0–1 | 1–2 | 15 | Pallister | 38,985 |
| 21 | A | Norwich C | 0–0 | 0–2 | 17 | | 17,370 |
| **February** | | | | | | | |
| 3 | H | Manchester | 0–0 | 1–1 | 17 | Blackmore | 40,274 |
| 10 | A | Millwall | 0–1 | 2–1 | 15 | Wallace, Hughes | 15,491 |
| 24 | A | Chelsea | 0–1 | 0–1 | 16 | | 29,979 |
| **March** | | | | | | | |
| 3 | H | Luton | 3–0 | 4–1 | 16 | McClair, Hughes, Wallace, Robins | 35,237 |
| 14 | H | Everton | 0–0 | 0–0 | 16 | | 37,398 |
| 18 | H | Liverpool | 0–1 | 1–2 | 16 | Whelan og | 46,629 |
| 21 | A | Sheffield Weds | 0–1 | 0–1 | 16 | | 33,260 |
| 24 | A | Southampton | 0–0 | 2–0 | 16 | Gibson, Robins | 20,510 |
| 31 | H | Coventry C | 2–0 | 3–0 | 16 | Hughes(2), Robins | 39,172 |
| **April** | | | | | | | |
| 14 | A | QPR | 0–1 | 2–1 | 14 | Robins, Webb | 18,997 |
| 17 | H | Aston Villa | 2–0 | 2–0 | 13 | Robins(2) | 44,080 |
| 21 | A | Tottenham H | 0–2 | 1–2 | 14 | Bruce pen | 33,317 |
| 30 | H | Wimbledon | 0–0 | 0–0 | 15 | | 29,281 |
| **May** | | | | | | | |
| 2 | A | Nottingham F | 0–4 | 0–4 | 16 | | 21,186 |
| 5 | H | Charlton Ath | 1–0 | 1–0 | 13 | Pallister | 35,389 |

## FA CUP

| Rnd | Date | Ven | Opponents | H/T | Res | Scorers | Att |
|-----|------|-----|-----------|-----|-----|---------|-----|
| 3 | 7 Jan | A | Nottingham F | 0–0 | 1–0 | Robins | 23,072 |
| 4 | 28 Jan | A | Hereford U | 0–0 | 1–0 | Blackmore | 13,777 |
| 5 | 18 Feb | A | Newcastle U | 1–0 | 3–2 | Robins, Wallace, McClair | 31,748 |
| 6 | 11 Mar | A | Sheffield U | 1–0 | 1–0 | McClair | 34,500 |
| s/f | 8 Apr | N | Oldham Ath | 1–1 | 3–3* | Robson, Webb, Wallace | 44,026 |
| Rep | 11 Apr | N | Oldham Ath | 0–0 | 2–1* | McClair, Robins | 35,005 |
| f | 12 May | W | C Palace | 1–1 | 3–3* | Robins, Hughes(2) | 80,000 |
| Rep | 17 May | W | C Palace | 0–0 | 1–0 | Martin | 80,000 |

## LITTLEWOODS CUP

| Rnd | Date | Ven | Opponents | H/T | Res | Scorers | Att |
|-----|------|-----|-----------|-----|-----|---------|-----|
| 2(1) | 20 Sep | A | Portsmouth | 3–0 | 3–2 | Ince(2), Wallace | 18,072 |
| 2(2) | 3 Oct | H | Portsmouth | 0–0 | 0–0 | | 26,698 |
| 3 | 25 Oct | H | Tottenham H | 0–1 | 0–3 | | 45,759 |

## LEAGUE GOAL-SCORERS 1989–90

| Mark Hughes | 13 | Arsenal [h], Millwall [h] (3), Manchester C [a], Coventry C [a] (2), Luton T [a], Wimbledon [a], Millwall [a], Luton T [h], Coventry [h] (2) |
|---|---|---|
| Mark Robins | 7 | Wimbledon [a], Luton T [h], Southampton [a], Coventry C [h], QPR [a], Aston Villa [h] (2) |
| Brian McClair | 5 | Arsenal [a], Everton [a], Southampton [h] (2), Luton T [h] |
| Danny Wallace | 3 | Luton T [a], Millwall [a], Luton T [h] |
| Steve Bruce | 3 | Arsenal [h], Coventry C [a], Tottenham H [a] (pen) |
| Gary Pallister | 3 | Nottingham F [h], Derby [h], Charlton Ath [h] |
| Bryan Robson | 2 | Crystal Palace [a], Millwall [h] |
| Russell Beardsmore | 2 | Everton [a], C Palace [h] |
| Clayton Blackmore | 2 | Luton T [a], Manchester C [h] |
| Neil Webb | 2 | Arsenal [h], QPR [a] |
| Lee Sharpe | 1 | Millwall [h] |
| Mike Phelan | 1 | Coventry [a] |
| Colin Gibson | 1 | Southampton [a] |
| Own goals | 1 | Whelan (v Liverpool [h]) |

46

## TOP TEN HOME ATTENDANCES

| 47,245 | v | Arsenal | Division 1 |
|---|---|---|---|
| 47,106 | v | Chelsea | Division 1 |
| 46,629* | v | Liverpool | Division 1 |
| 45,759 | v | Tottenham H | L'woods Cup 3rd Round |
| 44,080 | v | Aston Villa | Division 1 |
| 42,476 | v | Millwall | Division 1 |
| 41,492 | v | Sheffield Weds | Division 1 |
| 40,274** | v | Manchester C | Division 1 |
| 39,610 | v | Norwich C | Division 1 |
| 39,172 | v | Coventry C | Division 1 |

*Live television
**Restricted capacity for safety reasons

Mark Hughes – top League goal-scorer with 13.

## FA CUP GOAL-SCORERS 1989–90

| Mark Robins | 3 | Nottingham F [a], Newcastle U [a], Oldham Ath [s/f rep] |
|---|---|---|
| Brian McClair | 3 | Newcastle U [a], Sheffield U [a], Oldham Ath [s/f rep] |
| Mark Hughes | 2 | C Palace [f] |
| Danny Wallace | 2 | Newcastle [a], Oldham [s/f] |
| Bryan Robson | 2 | Oldham [s/f], Crystal Palace [f] |
| Neil Webb | 1 | Oldham [s/f] |
| Clayton Blackmore | 1 | Hereford [a] |
| Lee Martin | 1 | Crystal Palace [f rep] |

## LITTLEWOODS CUP GOAL-SCORERS 1989–90

| Paul Ince | 2 | Portsmouth [a] |
|---|---|---|
| Danny Wallace | 1 | Portsmouth [a] |

## ATTENDANCE RECORDS 1989–1990

|  | Total Home Attendances | Average Home Attendances |
|---|---|---|
| Football League | 740,248 | 38,960 |
| FA Cup | — |  |
| Littlewoods Cup (2) | 72,457 | 36,228 |
|  | **812,705** | **38,700** |

|  | Total Away Attendances | Average Away Attendances |
|---|---|---|
| Football League | 485,460 | 25,550 |
| FA Cup(8*) | 341,927 | 42,746 |
| Littlewoods Cup(1) | 18,072 | 18,072 |
|  | **845,459** | **30,194** |

*\* The FA Cup attendances include the semi-final (and replay) and final (and replay), which were played on neutral grounds.*

*Total League attendance: 1,225,708 (av 32,255) against 1988–1989 figure of 1,143,814 (av 30,100).*

*A total of 1,658,209 watched United games during the 1989–1990 season, both home and away (including the FA Cup final and replay), an average of 33,841 per game.*

## APPEARANCES AND GOAL-SCORERS 1989–1990

**League Appearances:** Phelan (38); McClair (37); Hughes (36 + 1 sub); Leighton (35); Pallister (35); Bruce (34); Martin (28 + 5 sub); Wallace (24 + 3 sub); Ince (24 + 2 sub); Robson (20); Blackmore (19 + 10 sub); Anderson (14 + 4 sub); Duxbury (13 + 8 sub); Sharpe (13 + 6 sub); Donaghy (12 + 3 sub); Robins (10 + 9 sub); Webb (10); Beardsmore (8 + 15 sub); Gibson (5 + 1 sub); Sealey (2); Bosnich (1); Milne (0 + 3 sub); Maiorana (0 + 2 sub); Brazil (0 + 1 sub); Graham (0 + 1 sub).

**League goal-scorers:** Hughes (13); Robins (7); McClair (5); Bruce (3 inc 1 pen); Pallister (3); Wallace (3); Beardsmore (2); Blackmore (2); Robson (2); Webb (2); Gibson (1); Phelan (1); Sharp (1); Own goals (1). **Total: 46.**

**Littlewoods Cup Appearances** (*Max 3*): Leighton (3); Donaghy (3); Phelan (3); Pallister (3); Robson (3); Ince (3); McClair (3); Hughes (3); Bruce (2); Wallace (2); Duxbury (1 + 2 sub); Sharpe (1 + 2 sub); Anderson (1); Martin (1); Beardsmore (1); Maiorana (1 sub); Blackmore (1 sub n/u).

**Littlewoods Cup Goal-scorers:** Ince (2); Wallace (1). **Total: 3.**

**FA Cup Appearances** (*Max 8*): Hughes (8); Martin (8); McClair (8); Pallister (8); Bruce (7); Leighton (7); Phelan (7); Ince (6 + 1 sub); Wallace (6 + 1 sub); Anderson (4); Robson (4); Webb (4); Robins (3 + 5 sub); Blackmore (2 + 2 sub); Duxbury (2 + 2 sub); Beardsmore (1 + 3 sub); Gibson (1 + 1 sub); Donaghy (1); Sealey (1); Milne (0 + 1 sub).

**FA Cup Goal-scorers:** McClair (3); Robins (3); Hughes (2); Wallace (2); Robson (2); Blackmore (1); Martin (1); Webb (1). **Total: 17.**

## RECORDS

**League performance:**

|  | P | W | D | L | F | A | Pts |
|---|---|---|---|---|---|---|---|
| Home | 19 | 8 | 6 | 5 | 26 | 14 | 30 |
| Away | 19 | 5 | 3 | 11 | 20 | 33 | 18 |

**Home wins against:** Arsenal, Millwall, Southampton, Nottingham F, Luton T, Coventry C, Aston Villa, Charlton Ath

**Away wins against:** Coventry C, Luton T, Millwall, Southampton, QPR

**Biggest win:** 5–1 v Millwall (home)

**Highest League attendance (home):** 47,245 v Arsenal

**Lowest League attendance (home):** 29,281 v Wimbledon

**Highest League attendance (away):** 43,246 v Manchester C

**Lowest League attendance (away):** 9,622 v Wimbledon

## BARCLAYS LEAGUE DIVISION 1
### Season 1989–1990

|  | P | W | D | L | F | A | Pts |
|---|---|---|---|---|---|---|---|
| Liverpool | 38 | 23 | 10 | 5 | 78 | 37 | 79 |
| Aston Villa | 38 | 21 | 7 | 10 | 57 | 38 | 70 |
| Tottenham H | 38 | 19 | 6 | 13 | 59 | 47 | 63 |
| Arsenal | 38 | 18 | 8 | 12 | 54 | 38 | 62 |
| Chelsea | 38 | 16 | 12 | 10 | 58 | 50 | 60 |
| Everton | 38 | 17 | 8 | 13 | 57 | 46 | 59 |
| Southampton | 38 | 15 | 10 | 13 | 71 | 63 | 55 |
| Wimbledon | 38 | 13 | 16 | 9 | 47 | 40 | 55 |
| Nottingham F | 38 | 15 | 9 | 14 | 55 | 47 | 54 |
| Norwich C | 38 | 13 | 14 | 11 | 44 | 42 | 53 |
| QPR | 38 | 13 | 11 | 14 | 45 | 44 | 50 |
| Coventry C | 38 | 14 | 7 | 17 | 39 | 59 | 49 |
| **MANCHESTER U** | **38** | **13** | **9** | **16** | **46** | **47** | **48** |
| Manchester C | 38 | 12 | 12 | 14 | 43 | 52 | 48 |
| C Palace | 38 | 13 | 9 | 16 | 42 | 66 | 48 |
| Derby Co | 38 | 13 | 7 | 18 | 43 | 40 | 46 |
| Luton T | 38 | 10 | 13 | 15 | 43 | 57 | 43 |
| Sheffield Weds | 38 | 11 | 10 | 17 | 35 | 51 | 43 |
| Charlton Ath | 38 | 7 | 9 | 22 | 31 | 57 | 30 |
| Millwall | 38 | 5 | 11 | 22 | 39 | 65 | 26 |